BAY OF PIGS

CIA'S CUBAN DISASTER, APRIL 1961

PHIL CARRADICE

Pen & Sword
MILITARY

First published in Great Britain in 2018 by
PEN AND SWORD MILITARY
an imprint of
Pen and Sword Books Ltd
47 Church Street
Barnsley
South Yorkshire S70 2AS

Copyright © Phil Carradice, 2018

ISBN 978 1 526728 29 6

Typeset by Aura Technology and Software Services, India
Maps by George Anderson
Printed and bound in Malta by Gutenberg

Pen & Sword Books Ltd incorporates the imprints of Pen & Sword
Archaeology, Atlas, Aviation, Battleground, Discovery, Family History, History, Maritime,
Military, Naval, Politics, Railways, Select, Social History, Transport, True Crime, Claymore Press,
Frontline Books, Leo Cooper, Praetorian Press, Remember When, Seaforth Publishing and Wharncliffe.

For a complete list of Pen and Sword titles please contact
Pen and Sword Books Limited
47 Church Street, Barnsley, South Yorkshire, S70 2AS, England
email: enquiries@pen-and-sword.co.uk
website: www.pen-and-sword.co.uk

CONTENTS

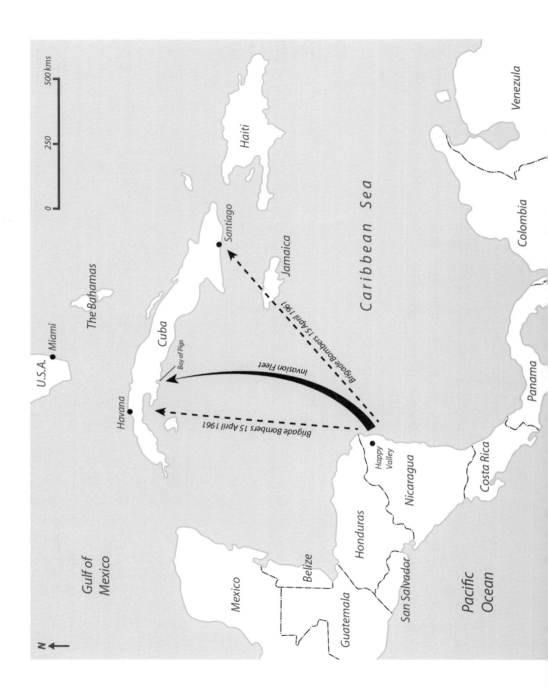

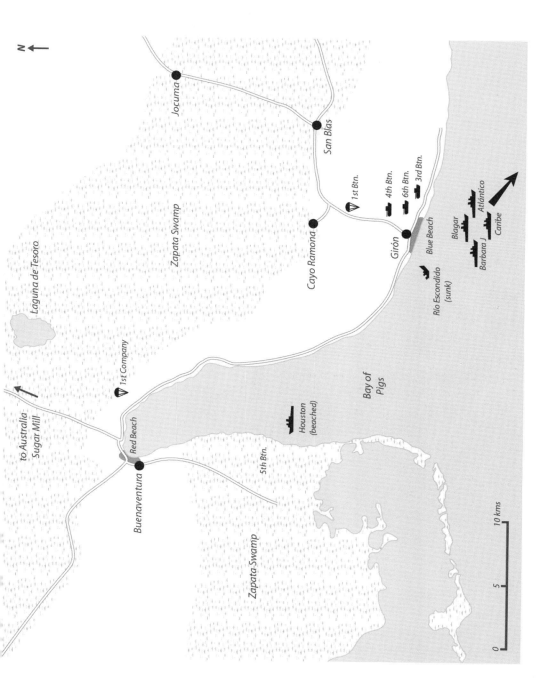

N

to Australia
Sugar Mill

Laguna de Tesoro

Buenaventura

Red Beach

1st Company

Zapata Swamp

Zapata Swamp

5th Btn.

Houston
(beached)

Bay of
Pigs

Cayo Ramona

Jocuma

San Blas

1st Btn.

4th Btn.

6th Btn.

3rd Btn.

Girón

Blue Beach

Río Escondido
(sunk)

Blagar

Atlántico

Barbara J

Caribe

10 kms

0   5

5

INTRODUCTION

'History never rests when it needs to tell the truth.'

Pepe San Román

As a teenager in the 1960s I guess I was like most adolescents, argumentative – even hostile – in my views about things like the use of nuclear weapons. I went on several Ban the Bomb marches and in the evenings I would sit for hours and argue with my father. He was happy to cross swords but whatever we discussed he was quite clear where his views lay: diametrically opposed to mine.

'That nuclear bomb you keep going on about,' I remember him saying when news about the Bay of Pigs first broke, 'is not as dangerous as you think. It's all that keeps the peace in this world.'

In Dad's view nobody would be stupid enough to push the button and send us all to oblivion. The bomb was a deterrent, pure and simple. It was a common enough point of view in those days and while I don't say I ever agreed with him, not then or now, it was an argument that could not be just brushed away like summer sand on the back porch.

Of course, what his argument did not allow for was the deranged psychopath who, when all was lost, would happily turn himself and the rest of the world to ash. That was a possibility that Dad would never acknowledge.

My father, born in the Depression years with Hitler and Stalin already girding their loins, had no time for appeasers. If there was someone out there who was prepared to flout the rules then Dad, not unlike JFK's Chiefs of Staff, I suppose, had only one response.

'Take them out!' he would declare and turn away, discussion over.

With views like that it was inevitable that his opinion of the seemingly regular clashes between the US and Cuba would be with the forces of conservatism. Where I saw Fidel and Che as harbingers of a new world, he regarded them as dangerous flouters of the traditional order.

The 1960s, perhaps more than any other ten-year span during the Cold War was, to misuse the lines of poet Jeff Nuttall, a time of Bomb Culture.

'Closest we ever came to nuclear war, boy,' my father exclaimed after the Bay of Pigs affair ended in what seemed like an American defeat.

He said the same thing the following year when the Cuban Missile Crisis was consigned to memory – except that this time he saw it as a US victory. In one respect I confess to partly agreeing with him: 1961 and 1962, two years when nuclear war could easily have erupted.

Partly agreed with him, yes but, as ever, the devil was in the detail. Dad was sure we did not go to war because of the presence of nuclear arsenals in the US and USSR. My view was the opposite: the world had been brought to the edge of destruction by those nuclear weapons he was so sure about. Everyone, I felt, would have been a lot safer without them.

'Full scale conventional war, boy,' Dad would exclaim time and time again. 'That's what would have happened without the bomb.'

He would fix me with a steely gaze, sniff derisively and point his pipe stem somewhere in the direction of my solar plexus. 'Just think what might have happened if Kennedy had sent the Marines into Cuba after that débâcle at the Bay of Pigs. Blood and guts everywhere.'

He would pause for a moment, then shake his head and move on. 'The Russians would have come in, then the Chinese. We'd have been dragged in too. If we'd banned the bomb, like you want, then there'd have been no ultimate deterrent so anybody could wage war when and where they liked. But fear of that last big bang, that's what kept us safe. Think about it, boy. Do you want to see millions of dead people – because that's what you'd have? Agreed?'

I didn't then and I don't think I do now. It remains a difficult question to answer and the jury, as they say, is still out on that particular issue. There was no convincing my father, however; he had no doubts.

And now, fifty or so years after those two seminal events of the Cold War I still have no clear answer to the dilemma. Could the Bay of Pigs disaster – and, because you cannot really separate the two, the 1962 Cuban Missile Crisis as well – have escalated into international conflict with nuclear holocaust waiting at the end?

Possibly. Khrushchev warned the US to back off in 1961 and went a stage further the following year. We were close and it took individuals of skill and bravery to get us through the troubles, whatever means they used. That's what makes the Bay of Pigs such an interesting topic.

The CIA-backed invasion could have succeeded – if Kennedy had not been so pre-occupied with plausible deniability. New Frontier, Camelot, whatever cliché they draped across his willing shoulders, it was something for which I have never been able to forgive him. So the Bay of Pigs adventure could have succeeded – couldn't it? Whether or not it should have is another matter.

At the end of the day it is down to people to make up their own minds. Weigh the evidence, study the events and characters, and give the topic the gravitas it deserves.

1. PERSPECTIVE

'How may I live without my name? I have given you my soul;
leave me my name.'

Arthur Miller, *The Crucible*

There are moments in history which, by virtue of the way in which we describe, log or name them, are instantly memorable. Sadly, the names we use to label the events are all too often more interesting than the actual occasions themselves.

The Defenestration of Prague is one. Over the years defenestration became something of a tradition in Prague, citizens showing their displeasure or opposition by hurling their political rulers out of the windows of the local castle. If the victims were lucky they would land on a dung heap or something soft. If not, like Jan Masaryk in 1948, '*C'est la guerre.*'

The War of Jenkins Ear sounds wonderful but in reality was little more than a series of skirmishes between trading vessels from Britain and Spain. The war began in 1739 when Captain Robert Jenkins had his ear cut off in a shipboard scuffle – and no, the severed ear was not presented to Parliament as popular sentiment would have us believe.

Despite its fascinating nomenclature, the Diet of Worms was nothing more than an assembly of the Holy Román Empire held in the Germanic city of Worms in 1521. Admittedly, Martin Luther was there to defend his position but nailing his Ninety-five Theses to the door of the Castle Church, Wittenberg was probably a lot more interesting. How did he do it, one nail in the corner or ninety-five separate pins?

The list is interminable. However, one of the few events that sounds fascinating when you first hear of it, yet still manages to live up to its potential is the sad and ultimately tragic fiasco of the Bay of Pigs Invasion.

A precursor to the Cuban Missile Crisis, it took place in 1961 and was an inept, entertaining and sometimes farcical attempt by the CIA to covertly design and implement an invasion of Cuba. The invasion would, it was hoped, spark a rising that would lead to the downfall of Cuban leader Fidel Castro.

Still renowned and commemorated in Cuba, the participants and events have faded from the memory of the general public in America and Britain. It is hardly surprising with popular opinion focusing on Kennedy's supposed victory in the

Playa Larga, Red Beach as it was called, the northernmost landing beach.

Cuban Missile Crisis the following year. The Bay of Pigs was a defeat, a spectacular defeat, a failure of mammoth proportions. Best consign it to those realms of glitches and failures that only surface in the midnight hours.

The Bay of Pigs was the USA's worst military disaster since the war of 1812 when British forces burned the White House. And, of course, there was more to come in the shape of the wrong war at the wrong time: the conflict in Vietnam. Yet the ramifications from the shambolic 1961 attempt to invade Cuba were equally as far-reaching.

If events at the Bay of Pigs have more in common with an episode of *Monty Python's Flying Circus* than they do with the 1945 invasion of Iwo Jima and the landing at Inchon during the war in Korea – both of which it was supposed to replicate – then that simply adds to the intrigue.

More importantly, it adds to the gung-ho foolishness of America's Central Intelligence Agency and the Joint Chiefs of Staff who were meant to oversee the plan and approve both its development and implementation.

The whole sorry episode was part of America's post-war paranoia about communism. At a time when self-aggrandisement and self-congratulation were part of the American people's belief in themselves as 'the policemen of the world', the spectre of creeping communism would not lie down and die.

Above all the débâcle revolved around the desire of America's leaders to maintain what was called 'plausible deniability'. Although funded by the US Treasury with soldiers trained and equipped by the CIA and the US military, the plan was presented to the world as an invasion cobbled together and led by Cuban exiles who had fled the island after Castro's revolution. These exiles, according to the deception, were now attempting to win back control of their homeland.

In reality, no one had to delve too deeply into the murky depths of the operation to realize that the dark hand of the CIA was immersed in the plan, right up to the armpits. To mix yet another metaphor into the catalogue of disasters, when the dust had cleared the CIA and, by default, the Kennedy administration as well, had received a very bloody nose.

The Bay of Pigs affair saw John F. Kennedy at his worst: lacking in judgement, naïve and ineffective. And while events may have occasionally descended into the hilarious humour of a Whitehall farce there is also a tragic side to the invasion. The landing on 17 April 1961, the military build-up in the weeks before and the dramatic days that followed have the tragi-comedy appeal that Shakespeare would have loved.

Over a hundred members of the invading exile army were killed before they could even get off the landing beaches or cross the wild Zapata swamplands. Many more, specially trained guerrilla fighters who had been sent ahead of the invasion to act as infiltrators, and locals who were regarded simply as potential collaborators, were rounded up and either shot or imprisoned by Castro's forces.

President John F Kennedy, young, dynamic – naïve and inexperienced.

Castro's militia, 200,000 part-time soldiers whose real occupations were jobs like teaching, cane cutting or charcoal burning, bore the brunt of the fighting around the killing grounds of Playa Girón and Playa Larga in the early hours of the first day. Attempting to support the regular Cuban Army, they took high casualties, possibly in the thousands. The figure has never been made totally clear.

However, the extensive casualty list acted, not as a deterrent for Castro's revolutionaries, but as a brilliant recruiting tool. He could not have planned it better. As an ironic Che Guevara wrote in a scribbled note to President Kennedy: 'Thanks for Playa Girón. Before the invasion, the revolution was weak. Now it is stronger than ever.'

If the Bay of Pigs was a 'coming of age' for Fidel, for Che and for the new regime, it was also a very definite wake-up call for the US. The disaster was a lesson learned even if it was one that Kennedy and his advisors would not have deliberately chosen: 'It was a horribly expensive lesson, but it was well learned. In later months the President's father would tell him that, in its perverse way, the Bay of Pigs was not a misfortune but a benefit.'

It is hard to see, fully, Joe Kennedy's logic and it is doubtful if JFK himself ever quite grasped what his father was trying to say. JFK could never get beyond the human cost. Joe, nothing if not a first-class pragmatist, was not concerned about people. Ideas and causes were his area of interest.

John F. Kennedy had inherited the operation from his predecessor, Dwight Eisenhower. The old victor of the Normandy landings was more than happy to leave the final decision on whether to launch or postpone the

Che Guevara, revolutionary icon.

12

invasion to his successor. According to Jack B. Pfeiffer: 'Following his initial interest in the developing program, President Eisenhower's personal involvement [had] dropped off sharply by the late summer of 1960.'

Perhaps realizing that Cuba was something of a poisoned chalice, Ike was certainly more interested in things like golf during the final days of his presidency. It might be an urban myth but for many years popular opinion held that the floor of the Oval Office behind the President's desk was pitted and indented by the spikes on Eisenhower's golf shoes where he had rushed in for a meeting after practising his shots on the White House lawn.

And while Kennedy might later lament that none of his advisors had attempted to stop him making foolish decisions, he learned from his mistakes. Perhaps that was what his father had been trying to tell him.

For some time after the failure JFK was depressed and unhappy. His wife Jackie and brother Bobby had never seen him so low. Always susceptible to bouts of poor health, there were serious concerns about what the stresses and strains of the presidency were doing to him. Time, however, was a good healer. A few weeks later, in a conversation with friend and journalist Ben Bradlee, JFK's humour and fighting spirit rose to the surface again. Like many of his supposedly off-the-cuff remarks, Kennedy's words to Bradlee were carefully thought out, laced with heavy irony and intended to make a point, as quoted by Dalleck: 'The first advice I'm going to give to my successor is to watch the generals and to avoid feeling that because they were military men their opinions on military matters were worth a damn!'

Joe Kennedy Snr, the dominating, and domineering, force behind the Kennedy family.

It was a stance that did not change throughout his remaining two years as president and was a significant factor in the way he handled the coming Cuban Missile Crisis.

Tragic, farcical, foolish, heroic – the fiasco at the Bay of Pigs was all of those things. Even the name, the Bay of Pigs – Cochinos Bay as the Cubans call it – has an element of farce about it, an element of farce that belies the tragedy of the whole affair.

Now, with hindsight, it seems almost inconceivable that such a plan could be devised and implemented. And, of course, it was the ordinary soldiers and patriots who suffered the most.

There are participants still alive – from both sides – men and women who might view the events of April 1961 with different perspectives but all of whom know that they took part in a dynamic and world-changing piece of history.

Perhaps the greatest sadness in the whole affair came with the unchallengeable belief of the Cuban exiles that the USA would send in troops to help them once the beachhead had been established. Many of the Brigade members put it on record that CIA operatives had promised help. That may have been the case but it was not, and never had been, the view of the men in charge.

A Cuban sugar plantation in the nineteenth century. (Library of Congress)

The pace of life in Cuba has changed little over the ages. Here a fisherman tries his luck with a hand line. (Photo Trudy Carradice)

Kennedy, like Eisenhower before him, was adamant that no US soldiers would ever be used. In late March 1961, as quoted by Schlesinger, he told a press conference: 'There will not be, under any conditions, an intervention in Cuba by the United States Armed Forces ... The basic issue in Cuba is not one between the United States and Cuba. It is between the Cubans themselves.'

They were laudable words, carefully chosen by JFK, which undoubtedly summed up the attitudes of both the Kennedy and Eisenhower regimes. Perhaps inevitably, the Cuban exiles who were soon to risk their lives on the beaches around the Bay of Pigs chose not to believe him. That may well have been the workings of the closed minds of driven patriots but the Cuban exiles would not have arrived at that conclusion alone. There had to have been American promises made, if only by the culpable officers of the CIA.

The real tragedy of the Bay of Pigs was that no matter what happened on the invasion beaches, it was an operation doomed to fail. Grayston Lynch, one of only two Americans to go ashore with the soldiers of Brigade 2506, admirably summed it up: '2506 Assault Brigade fought hard to prevent this disaster but, as we were to discover later, no amount of effort on its part could have prevented it, for this invasion was doomed long before the men of the Brigade first sighted the dim outlines of Cochinos Bay.'

Three days in April, a time to live and a time to die; three days when the Cuban exiles of Brigade 2506 felt betrayed and abandoned by a global super power that had the strength and capability but not the inclination to help them in their hour of need; three days in April that should never be forgotten.

2. BACKGROUND TO DISASTER

'A revolution without firing squads is meaningless.'

Vladimir Ilyich Lenin

Fidel Castro seized control of Cuba at the beginning of 1959 when he and his rebel army supplanted the American-backed dictator Fulgencio Batista. Castro's revolution had huge popular support but in the turbulent world of Cuban politics that meant very little.

It was January 1959 and there was every reason to believe that he and his 26th of July Movement would soon go the way of so many other revolutionary groups. All too often would-be saviours had come to power swearing to bring dramatic change for the people of Cuba and then quickly reneged on their promises in the face of easy riches and sudden glory.

For years the island had been a hot-bed of revolution, of political assassination and corrupt practices. The public did not have to look very far for examples. In the wake of Castro's victory Batista fled to the Dominican Republic, a lucky and

Fulgencio Batista, the hated and venal American-backed president of Cuba – getting rid of him was Fidel Castro's first aim.

brilliantly timed escape that took him out of the hands of the revolutionary guerrillas and the Cuban people who would have happily strung him up from the nearest lamppost.

Batista had one thing to console him in his exile: stashed in his suitcases were around $300 million dollars, a huge fortune that he had amassed during his time in power. So why should this latest regime be any different? The answer was simple: previous revolutions had not had the magnetic, enigmatic and enthusiastic Fidel Castro at their head.

Castro had been involved in revolutionary politics since his time as a law student at Havana University. By nature a supporter of left wing ideals, he was not at this stage the communist that many people thought they saw. He was, however, quite happy to be regarded as a man of the people and was willing to resort to violence if he thought it would help fulfil his aims.

It had been a hard road to power. In July 1953 a failed assault on the Moncada Barracks in Santiago de Cuba had seen Fidel and his brother Raúl imprisoned for fifteen years on Cuba's penal colony, the Isle of Pines. Strangely, given what was about to happen, the Castro brothers were granted amnesty after serving just two years of their sentence.

If Batista had thought his clemency might have helped Castro change his ways he was proved wrong. Violence immediately erupted in Havana and by July, less than two months after the Castro brothers' release, the city was proving to be a very dangerous place to linger. Fearing assassination, Fidel and Raúl left Cuba before the end of the month, taking refuge in Mexico where they met Ernesto 'Che' Guevara and began recruiting and training a guerrilla army for the express purpose of removing Batista from power.

The story of Fidel Castro's return to Cuba, his two-year military campaign from the hills and forests of the Sierra Maestra that culminated with Batista's flight on New Year's Day 1959 are well known. The dictator's abrupt departure left the island without government or leadership for three days – not that Batista cared a great deal: he had his money and he had escaped with his life.

Just prior to Castro's triumphal entry into Havana on 5 January, Manuel Urrutia Lleo was installed as president with José Miro Cardona as prime minister. It was intended to be a moderate government that would control things during what was clearly a transitional period but, even so, Cardona announced the appointment of the decidedly radical Fidel Castro as head of the Cuban armed forces. Everyone knew where the power lay and, inevitably, members of Castro's 26th of July Movement – named in honour of the unsuccessful attack on Moncada Barracks – took the main ministerial posts in the new government.

Already exceeding his position as head of the armed forces, Castro was soon dismissing the idea of democratic elections. The new leadership would be an example of what he called 'direct democracy' where the Cuban people could express their will in direct fashion at mass demonstrations and public gatherings, thus making traditional voting obsolete.

Castro's concept of direct democracy was hugely popular in some quarters but was viewed with suspicion and cynicism in others. If Batista's rule had been a one-man dictatorship, many believed that their new leaders (effectively Fidel Castro) were intent on establishing a similar regime. Consequently, almost from

Raúl Castro and Che Guevara, in earlier days.

Brothers Fidel and Raúl Castro, visiting troops in the field.

the beginning Fidel was forced to deal with significant opposition, both internally and from abroad.

Very quickly, he discovered that the men from his rebel army might have made good guerrilla fighters but they had little or no idea how to govern a country. After only a few short months those who were incompetent or incapable of changing were dismissed; Fidel's brother Raúl and Che Guevara were two of the top echelon with whom Castro kept faith.

In the early summer of 1959 Fidel went one stage further when he removed the president and took complete control himself. Bowing to the constitution he did appoint a nominal figurehead, a 'puppet President' in the shape of

Fidel Castro, revolutionary, guerrilla fighter and future ruler of Cuba

pliable Osvaldo Dortico, a lawyer who held distinctly communist views but was unlikely to interfere with Fidel's plans in any way.

Getting rid of the detritus from Batista's rule was something that the Cuban people demanded and if Fidel was intent on maintaining his popularity with the masses this was not something he could afford to ignore. There were still dozens of men on the island who had, on Batista's orders, been involved in the torture and execution of political opponents and of ordinary members of the public.

Revenge was in the air and, sensing the mood, Castro set up show trials, followed by almost 500 executions. Huge numbers of people attended to listen to and watch the proceedings many of which were held in sports stadiums or arenas. These mass hearings were arguably the twentieth-century equivalent of the Salem witch trials or even public persecutions in front of the plebeians in the Román amphitheatre.

Critics, particularly in the US, were vocal in their condemnation of the trials, declaring that they were not fair representations of justice. Newspaper headlines from all parts of the country roared that the new Cuban government seemed to be more interested in vengeance than in justice. In response Castro was emphatic – revolutionary justice was based on moral conviction, not legal case studies or the finer precepts of law.

Physical torture, as used by Batista, was ruled out but Castro allowed psychological punishments such as solitary confinement, starvation diets and threats against prisoners and their families. Press censorship was introduced at the beginning of 1960 after the owners of the Cuban newspapers, by nature solidly conservative, began to object to the leftward swing of the new regime.

Fidel seemed to be involved in every aspect of government, his huge reserves of energy driving him forward. His hands-on approach was productive. In front of 17,000 spectators in the Sports Palace Stadium in Havana, the trial of men accused of a bombing outrage returned a not guilty verdict. Castro saw the danger and ordered a retrial. This second time, much to the appreciation of the spectators, the accused were found guilty and sentenced to life imprisonment.

Despite the popularity of the trials and executions a significant ground swell of opposition remained and Castro was soon faced by an upsurge of military activity from various counter-revolutionary groups. These were usually ex-Batista supporters or disaffected citizens who doubted the integrity of the new government. Many of them, taking a leaf out of Castro's book, set up bases for guerrilla

When Batista fled at the beginning of 1959 he had with him millions of dollars stashed in a suitcase: the clichéd Latin-American tinpot dictator.

operations in the rugged Escambray Mountains. From there they waged what was to become a six-year war against the new regime.

The dissidents received substantial funding from various sources. To begin with there were the exiled Cuban groups, men and women who had fled the island when Castro came to power. Many of them were formerly wealthy farmers and businessmen who, with the arrival of Castro and the move away from private ownership, suddenly saw their land appropriated and profit margins slashed. From the safety of Miami they were happy to lend financial support to the 'new rebels'.

Right-wing governments from nearby Caribbean islands like the Dominican Republic also gave assistance, usually in the form of arms and equipment. The most significant supporter of the Escambray dissidents, however, was the US Central Intelligence Agency.

The CIA had been founded in 1947 as a clandestine organization whose original aim was to counter the activities of Russia's KGB. Gradually the role of this secretive agency expanded to include helping military and political causes that were considered useful or advantageous to the US.

As the Cold War developed the role of the CIA became ever more important. No longer was it considered good enough to send in a gunboat whenever there was trouble. That way lay war and huge expenditure on arms, weapons and personnel. Now, approaches had to be more imaginative and subtle. They had, in fact, to be covert. Enter the CIA.

Even though he had acknowledged Castro's regime within days of the revolution, President Dwight Eisenhower had always viewed Cuba's new rulers with suspicion. Despite Fidel's unexpected but enormously popular tour of the US in the spring of 1960, the fear of what Eisenhower's administration insisted was a communist regime just ninety miles from Florida seemed to imbue almost every American thought and deed during the final days of Ike's presidency.

Castro was consistent in his denials. He was not, he said, a communist. His agrarian reforms (mainly nationalization of farm land) and the Marxist education camps he had created since coming to power were for the benefit of the people, not some esoteric idea. He did not see – or claimed not to see – the problem.

Even so, Eisenhower managed to avoid encountering him – after all, this was not a formal state visit, Castro having arrived unannounced – by arranging to play golf on his favourite course at Augusta during the time Fidel was in Washington. It was left to Vice-President Richard Nixon to formally greet and meet with Castro on Capitol Hill.

Left: Dwight Eisenhower, hero of the Normandy landings and president of the USA.

Below: Brothers in arms – Fidel at left, Che centre, parade through Havana after seizing power.

A three-hour meeting of bluster and counter-bluster was followed by Fidel's complaint that Nixon browbeat him, lectured him and treated him like a school-boy. Following Fidel's departure the vice-president sent a memo to Eisenhower stating that either Castro was incredibly naïve or he was showing an amazing degree of communist discipline. Either way, he was trouble and at some stage would have to be dealt with.

There is a temptation to conclude that the decision to oust Castro came like a bolt of lightning to Eisenhower. But this was no sudden whim, this was a gradual progression, fuelled by Fidel's thoughts and actions and by America's view of itself as the protector of western civilization.

It could all have been very different. Castro came back from his trip to America with mixed feelings about his capitalist neighbour. He was, at least, prepared to work with them and that October he even went so far as to host a meeting of nearly 2,000 American travel agents with a view to promoting Cuba as a tourist paradise.

Eisenhower meets Richard Nixon, his vice-president, and the Nixon family.

American paranoia soon put a stop to that. Castro had been negotiating with Great Britain to buy military jets until Eisenhower persuaded the British to stall on the deal. Castro was furious. He began to vacillate, his mercurial and unstable temperament taking him first one way then the other. Finally he decided that his best course of action would be to use the US as a whipping boy to distract attention from any shortcomings in his own policies.

It was a sensible ploy and America fell neatly into Castro's web of confusion. The fear of what Fidel and his country could become, rather than what they were now, was intense and soon developed into an almost pathological hatred of Cuba's leader.

That October, as the US travel agents were still enjoying Castro's hospitality, matters came to a head. An unexpected and unofficial leaflet drop on Havana by a Cuban exile flying from Florida in an old Second World War bomber brought sudden confusion to the city. The aircraft was fired at by Cuban anti-aircraft gunners as it buzzed, low and menacing, across Havana. The plane dropped only paper but falling shrapnel from the AA shells and machine-gun rounds were the probable cause of a number of injuries to the public. There were even four deaths.

The leaflet drop and the resultant deaths provoked an immediate response from the Cuban leader. That night Fidel gave a two-hour television broadcast, speaking vehemently and, as usual, without notes. Four days later, on 26 October 1959, he called a mass rally. Thousands turned up to hear their leader as the American travel agents quickly gathered together their bottles of Havana Club rum, souvenirs of their visit, and headed for their waiting planes.

The rally opened with Fidel making a theatrical arrival in a helicopter, leaping from the machine almost before it landed, clutching a rifle in his hand and dressed in his traditional army fatigues. The crowd was ecstatic. The dramatic beginning was followed by blame for the deaths being laid firmly at the door of the US.

Fidel went on to make the most significant anti-American diatribe he had ever given. In that instant all remaining hopes of a peaceful and mutually beneficial existence were gone. From here on it was just a matter of time before serious trouble erupted.

Apart from the belligerent remarks of Cuba's leader, when they looked at the regime and at events on the island US advisors and diplomats shuddered. They could see only the traditional apparatus of Bolshevism – a single-party state, trade unions under government control, restriction of free speech and heavy-handed shackles on press freedom.

There was a plan, they felt, to use Cuba to spread communist revolution across Latin-America. The architect of such a plan was not made clear although there were already concerns that with Castro moving further to the left, Nikita Khrushchev and the Soviet bloc might soon be making overtures to Cuba. In fact Castro had, unbeknown to the Americans, already signed a trade agreement with Moscow.

What had become obvious to everyone was that Fidel Castro would not go away; therefore it was up to the US, with or without support from other nations, to take direct action in order to get rid of him. Otherwise his influence would be too powerful as outlined in a later CIA investigation: 'Castro's leadership constitutes a real menace capable of eventually overthrowing the elected governments in any one or more of the weak Latin-American republics.'

His visit to the US had taught Fidel a lot about the Americans. He began to see their hand – admittedly a disguised hand often wrapped up in the glove of the CIA – in many of the problems that beset the world. He was already being seriously courted for more than just trade agreements by representatives of the Soviet Union and his opinion of America began to harden into active dislike. One of his most famous slogans dates from around this time: 'Cuba si, Yanquis no'.

A mighty pairing, Castro and Khrushchev – an early propaganda poster.

As Castro's views on America became more vocal and aggressive, they were mirrored by a number of attacks by Cuban exiles on Havana and the surrounding countryside. Fields of sugarcane and their refining mills were obvious targets for the attacks. Many of these attacks came from the air, exile pilots flying old Second World War bombers from airfields – there were nearly 200 of them – in nearby Florida. And while such attacks were not American there was no denying the 'Yanqui' support and encouragement.

In March 1960 the French cargo ship *La Coubre*, waiting to discharge her cargo of weapons and ammunition recently bought from Belgium, blew up and sank in Havana harbour. Eighty Cuban dockers and workers died in the explosion, well over a hundred were seriously wounded and Castro immediately blamed the US. There was no proof but the CIA and Cuban exiles from America were felt to be heavily involved.

Tension between the two countries was further intensified in June 1960 when a number of Soviet tankers full of Russian oil arrived in Havana. After taking advice from the US government, Texaco, Esso and several smaller oil companies refused to offload and refine the product, setting into motion a domino string of responses.

It might have been a knee-jerk reaction but there was no way Fidel was ever going to meekly accept the decision of the oil companies. In retaliation he nationalized all of the US-controlled refineries on the island.

Furious at Fidel's seizure of prime US assets, Eisenhower responded by placing a partial ban on Cuba's vitally important sugar trade with America. Castro's reply? Nationalization of over 500 US and private businesses on the island. These included companies like the Coca-Cola bottling plant, the telephone company, banks and, inevitably, the sugar mills.

Not to be outdone, a full US ban on Cuba's sugar imports into the USA was promptly issued by President Eisenhower.

When Castro and Eisenhower had finished spiting each other, Fidel found himself faced by possible ruin. The sale of sugar had always been crucially important to Cuba's farmers and now the most lucrative market in the western world was being denied to them.

Salvation came in the squat, bulky but politically astute form of Nikita Khrushchev. Castro and the Soviet premier immediately thrashed out a deal that saw the Soviet Union buy the vast bulk of Cuban sugar. Without realizing it, American attempts at controlling Fidel had achieved nothing more than to push him firmly into the waiting arms of the Soviet Union.

It was time for America to think again. Over the previous decade Eisenhower and CIA Director Allen Dulles had developed considerable experience in the

The French freighter *La Coubre*, destroyed by bombs in Havana harbour in March 1960

business of covert operations. In 1953 and 1954, they had used the CIA's Directorate of Plans to design and then implement revolutions to replace unfriendly governments in Iran and Guatemala. And it was the Directorate of Plans that now took the lead in the projected overthrow of Fidel Castro.

Allen Dulles, having on 13 January 1960 gained approval from the National Security Council to begin covert action against Cuba, set things in motion. During the winter of 1960 the CIA Directorate began to formulate ideas for Fidel's downfall.

Plans to assassinate the Cuban leader were drawn up, methods ranging from the use of rifles with telescopic sights to dosing his food with LSD, from an exploding sea shell to gifts of diving suits coated in poison. The spectre of James Bond fantasies was, it seemed, alive and kicking in the hallowed halls of Washington DC.

There was even contact between the CIA and gangsters like Johnny Rosselli and Sam Giancana. If the mob would agree to 'take out' Castro they would be rewarded by reclaiming all the lucrative gambling contracts and monopolies they had lost after the Cuban revolution. The plan came to nothing but it did not stop the CIA scheming.

Allen Dulles had delegated the task of eliminating Castro to Richard Bissell, Deputy Director for Plans in the CIA. Bissell was regarded as a brilliant organizer of covert missions, having been heavily involved in the recent Guatemala affair, and obviously possessed significant intelligence

President Kennedy and
Allen Dulles, Director of
the CIA

and ability. Unfortunately he was also obstinate and unbending. The writer
Jim Rasenberger summed him up when he claimed that Bissell had 'an excep-
tional intellect combined with a predilection for action. As the tough-talking
Kennedys would have put it – Bissell himself was too polite to use such language – he combined brains with balls.'

Having been given the task of developing the CIA plan, Richard Bissell put
together the Cuba Task Force, Branch 4 of the Western Hemisphere Division or
WH/4 as it was known. This unit included many of the men who had worked
with Bissell in the overthrow of Guatemala's president in 1954. To begin with
Bissell and many of the others believed that overthrowing Castro would be as
easy as getting rid of the Guatemala regime, failing to appreciate that the Cuban
leader possessed something Jacobo Arbenz of Guatemala had not even considered: popularity among his people.

Bissell's choice as first assistant or right-hand man was Tracy Barnes, a long-
time friend and colleague. Barnes was popular, a man with great social skills, but
he could certainly not be ranked as a first-rate thinker. He had been Bissell's chief
during the Guatemalan revolution but now the positions were reversed. Neither
man seemed unduly upset by the switch.

Jacob Esterline, an experienced CIA operative, was brought back from what he regarded as unpleasant and pointless duty in Venezuela. When he returned he was installed to run the day-to-day operations of the anti-Castro groups.

Long-time CIA agent Gerry Droller was enrolled, charged with finding and developing links with Cubans living in America. Howard Hunt, later to achieve some kind of publicity for his part in the Watergate Scandal, was also involved. His job was to assemble a Cuban government in exile.

David Phillips had used radio propaganda broadcasts during the Guatemala operation, convincing Jacobo Arbenz and his supporters that a ragtag gathering of rebels was actually a superbly trained army of several thousand. He was instructed to replicate the feat in Cuba.

In the first few months of 1960, working from Quarters Eye, a small wooden building situated close to the Lincoln Memorial in Washington, these men and others began to formulate their ideas. Gradually a plan of action was drawn up.

On 17 March the CIA's proposal was ready to be presented to President Eisenhower and the US National Security Council. It was explicit and dramatic

Jacob Esterline who had daily running of the plan.

with the single aim of destroying Fidel Castro. His regime was to be replaced with one that was more acceptable to the Cuban people – and of course to the US.

Significantly, the plan was to avoid any US connection, the first hard evidence of the theory of plausible deniability that was to haunt the administrations of both Dwight Eisenhower and JFK.

Rasenberger mentions that according to the proposal, in order to bring about Castro's removal it would be necessary to follow four essential action points:

1. to create a viable, unified and credible political opposition to Castro, working for the moment from exile in the USA,
2. to build up well-trained and powerful paramilitary forces, again outside Cuba,
3. to develop a covert intelligence network on the island, one that would feed information both into and out of Cuba,
4. to launch a stream of anti-Castro propaganda through things like leaflet drops and the development of medium wave radio broadcasts.

At this stage there was no mention of an invasion. If that became necessary then it did not take the most diligent of readers to see that the possibility had already been hinted at in the creation of paramilitary forces.

Such an intervention, if it came, would not be by the US. Rather, 'A Program of Covert Action Against the Castro Regime' put down a crucial marker. Any attacks or assaults on the island of Cuba would be carried out by Cuban nationals.

Paramilitary troops trained in guerrilla tactics would light the fuse of rebellion against Fidel Castro and America would not be implicated in any way. That, at least, was the plan as outlined by the CIA in March 1960.

President Eisenhower gave his approval. Almost before they knew it, the proposal to depose Fidel Castro had become official US policy. A few months later, on 18 August 1960, Eisenhower allocated a budget of $13 million for the operation. The die was set, there could be no going back and the fates of many hundreds of men and women were sealed that summer day in 1960.

3. PLANNING, REHEARSING AND CHANGING TO PLAN B

> 'How do I know what to do? I'm making this up as I go along.'
> Indiana Jones, *Raiders of the Lost Ark*

From the beginning it was obvious that the CIA's plan was in difficulty. Even the first stage of gathering together a unified political opposition to the Cuban regime was problematic. As Gerry Droller and Howard Hunt soon discovered, there were so many exile groups, all with different agendas and views of how to deal with Fidel Castro.

Despite constant quarrelling and sniping between the Cuban exiles, Frente Revolucionario Democrático, the FRD or the Front as it was known, was eventually pulled together. It was initially made up from five different anti-Castro underground organizations: the Revolutionary Rescue Movement, the Movement of Revolutionary Recovery, the Christian Democratic Movement, Triple A and Montecristi. Other groups like the People's Revolutionary Movement and the Student Revolutionary Directorate also soon threw their weight behind the new organization.

The more radical Cuban exiles, people such as Manuel Ray – 'Fidelismo without Fidel' as his brand of revolutionary politics was called – were not included. Ray and others were not ideologically opposed to Castro; they were bitter because he was running the country, not them. Publicly, at least, these were not the type of political exiles the CIA wanted.

Representatives of the original five groups making up the FRD, led by Dr Manuel Francisco Artime of the Revolutionary Rescue Movement, were presented to the public on 20 July 1960. The CIA controllers stayed well out of the way, determined to make this seem a purely Cuban affair.

The cover story that the exiles were operating on behalf of a rich, eccentric businessman who simply wanted to fight communism fooled nobody, not even the exiles themselves. Gleefully, the recruits called their supposed benefactor 'Uncle Sam'. They knew that no single individual would ever be wealthy enough to fund the invasion of a foreign country. The power behind the throne had to be America.

With 'branch' offices in several Latin American countries – established mainly to disguise the link with the US – the FRD was initially based in Mexico City but

John F. Kennedy is presented with the Brigade flag by Erneido Oliva Gonzalez as Manuel Artime looks on.

with Mexican authorities being unhelpful and more than a little suspicious of their uninvited guests, the Cuban exiles soon returned to Miami.

As Howard Hunt later explained, it was easy to get the leaders of the FRD to meet, getting them to agree with each other was virtually impossible. This was particularly the case where money was concerned: 'They asked for a monthly budget of $435,000 for activities abroad; $200,000 to increase operations in Cuba; and around $105,000 for a contingency fund, salaries and the Front's office expenses – a total of around $740,000.'

By the summer of 1960, regardless of the unreasonable demands for more money, the FRD was at least up and running. While its leaders travelled the world looking for support, Richard Bissell and his team from WH/4 continued to organize the forthcoming interventions. They were on a tight schedule, Dulles and Bissell having promised Eisenhower that everything would be finalized and ready within eight months. Already that was beginning to look like wishful thinking.

Finding and enlisting appropriate recruits for the paramilitary units had proceeded far slower than anyone expected but Droller, known to the Cubans by his work name of Frank Bender, stuck to his task. Early recruiting took place in Miami in April 1960, many of those who enlisted having been officers in Batista's army. Others were members of counter-revolutionary groups from within Cuba, men who had been head hunted specifically to join the new paramilitary units. Students and disgruntled exiles made up the remainder.

The first group of ten recruits left their safe house in the Homestead area south of Miami on 19 May. They were followed by a second group, again just ten in number, two days later. A five-hour road trip took both groups to Fort Myers on the coast of Florida. From there motorboats ferried them out to CIA-owned Useppa Island. It was isolated but had once been a holiday resort and boasted tennis courts and a dilapidated golf course.

Over the coming weeks more would-be soldiers arrived until there were over sixty men on the island. They stayed there for six weeks, undergoing examinations to measure their skills, personalities and intelligence. There were lie-detector tests to establish their trustworthiness but above all they were grilled on their political stance, interrogators repeatedly asking them for their views on communism, whether they had ever read Marxist literature and other supposedly revealing questions.

Revolutionaries Raúl Castro, Vilma Espín Guillois (feminist and chemical engineer married to Raúl), Jorge Risquet and José Nivaldo Causse, seen here in 1958.

In between the tests American instructors from Special Forces – all the while swearing that the operation had nothing to do with the US – trained them in guerrilla warfare, in amphibious assault techniques and in the use of radio equipment.

Relations between the US and Cuba deteriorated that summer, a situation that did not go unnoticed in the rest of the world. Nikita Khrushchev, in a speech to a Russian teachers' conference on 9 July, gave the US a clear warning: the Soviet Union would be supplying Fidel Castro with weapons, everything from small arms to aircraft, in an effort to support the Cuban revolution: 'The United States is now not at such an inaccessible distance from the Soviet Union as formerly ... if need be Soviet artillerymen can support the Cuban people with their rocket fire, should the aggressive forces in the Pentagon dare to start intervention against Cuba.'

With numbers on Useppa Island increasing daily, the early recruits were moved to two US military bases close to the Panama Canal for more training in the use of explosives, sabotage and psychological warfare. After that they were flown to Guatemala where the friendly government allowed them to take over a 5,000-acre ranch and coffee plantation on the side of a volcano in the Sierra Madre. More recruits soon joined them.

Conditions in this new camp were crude. There were no showers or recreational facilities and the men had to build themselves huts and latrines. The real name of the area was Helvetia but the CIA and the Cubans called it Base Trax.

Richard Nixon and Nikita Khrushchev, the best of enemies.

Thirty miles away in Retalhuleu the CIA also built an airstrip to act as an operational base for the aircraft that were to be used to support the guerrilla fighters.

Originally intended to be only a minor part of the operation, by the late summer of 1960 it was clear that aircraft would be expected to play a much more significant role than was first thought, as a later CIA investigation revealed: 'In addition to the need for aircraft for infiltration, propaganda and supply drops to dissident groups within Cuba, additional air transport capability would be required to move bodies and equipment to training sites outside the continental USA.'

The first group of forty-four pilots arrived in Guatemala at the end of August, a second group of fourteen joining them in September. The pilots were all Cuban, either ex-military or civilian flyers. They were instructed by Americans in how to fly the Douglas C-54 Skymasters and Douglas B-26 Invaders that had been allocated to them and almost immediately there was trouble.

The Cuban pilots and aircrews were all very conscious of rank, status and position. They felt that they were being patronized by their American comrades, many of whom did not speak Spanish with the result that much of the instruction had to be carried out by hand signals.

The Americans did, indeed, look down on the Cuban pilots, criticizing their ability and keeping themselves segregated with separate club facilities that remained closed to all Cubans. At one stage a message was posted on the noticeboard demanding that the Cuban flyers act like 'officers and gentlemen'. Things became so bad that many Cubans threatened to leave the training camp at Retalhuleu and several pilots did actually return to Miami in disgust.

Training for the guerrillas continued, long hours of weapons instruction and hikes to keep the men fit. On 7 September one of the recruits, a youngster called Carlos Rafael Santana, fell into a ravine and was killed. His serial number was 2506 and, in his honour, the exile force was christened Brigade 2506.

The aim of the paramilitary unit had always been to carry out guerrilla warfare. While the men of Brigade 2506 had been well-schooled in such techniques they could not hope to succeed in their mission without linking up with insurgent fighters in Cuba. Admiral Arleigh Burke, Chief of Navy Operations and a rabid anti-communist told John F. Kennedy that 'The plan was dependent on a general uprising in Cuba, and that the entire operation would fail without such an uprising.'

Unfortunately, the insurgents fighting in the Escambray Mountains, where the guerrilla campaign was to be waged, were being increasingly harried or eliminated by Castro's forces. These insurgent groups, the CIA learned, were neither as numerous nor as effective as they had been led to believe.

Supplies airlifted in by the CIA and the Cuban pilots recruited to Brigade 2506 often fell into the hands of the Cuban militia. The CIA later revealed that out of sixty-eight missions from September 1960 onward, only seven drops put the supplies where they were intended to go: 'Some of the American personnel involved in air operations still believe that some of the Cubans discharged their cargoes into the sea at the first opportunity and spent the time "tooling" around until the fuel gauges indicated that it was time to return to base.'

Castro's state police had become particularly efficient in sniffing out counter-revolutionaries in the cities while the army and militia carried out similar roles in the hinterland. Opposition to Fidel consisted of small groups who were poorly supplied and led. Their ability to arrange and carry out effective strikes against government forces were limited and their loyalty was questionable with individuals and whole groups quite likely to change allegiance at a whim. Clearly, the popularity of Fidel's regime was not as fragile as had been previously imagined.

By the end of November 1960 the Brigade was ready. The situation on Cuba, however, was increasingly uncertain with the capability of the rebel groups now a significant issue.

It was not just the Cuban insurgent groups: the pilots of the Brigade's air force were also struggling to grasp the finer points of the B-26 bombers. As the year drew to a close the CIA reluctantly noted that while ten B-26 aircraft had been provided for Brigade use, less than half a dozen of the Cuban pilots had any idea how to fly them.

Manuel Gonzales, one of the most experienced of the exile Cuban pilots, managed to make such a rough landing that his aircraft was badly damaged. He

The Frente leaders pose with Bobby Kennedy. From left: Roberto San Román, Manuel Artime, Ramon Ferrer, Kennedy, Enrique Ruiz-Williams, Pepe San Román and Erneido Oliva Gonzalez.

severely injured his diaphragm in the crash with the result that both he and his aircraft were lost to the operation.

Another aircraft under the control of the experienced Alvarez Builla and a crew with 45,000 flying hours between them, dropped their supply load not on the city of Trinidad but on a nearby power plant and then had to make an emergency landing in Mexico. The aircraft was confiscated and the crew interned. Accidents like these did not help with the standing of the Cubans in American eyes and, inevitably, they meant losses in personnel and equipment for the Brigade.

While still committed to the idea of neutralizing Castro, Bissell and Jacob Esterline were now faced with an unpalatable decision. The proposed guerrilla campaign was increasingly unrealistic. What should they do? There was only one possible solution: a traditional infantry landing from the sea. That was not something the Cuban exiles had been trained for but Dulles, Bissell, Esterline and others felt that they had no alternative.

In early November a message was sent to Trax Base from CIA headquarters in Langley, just outside Washington. Guerrilla training was to be suspended and, instead, members of Brigade 2506 were to be prepared for conventional seaborne landings.

The Brigade was immediately divided into battalions and companies with only eighty men retaining the role of infiltrators and saboteurs. These would-be infiltrators were immediately sent for further training and selection at San José de Buenavista Farm, well away from the assault battalions. Here their numbers were reduced to just thirty.

The idea of a rising by Cuban dissidents had not totally evaporated. The new scheme called for a significant number of assault troops from Brigade 2506 to establish a beachhead close to the Escambray Mountains where, despite their inadequacies, rebel groups were known to be operating. With the aid of the thirty-odd infiltrators the CIA clung to the hope that these dissidents might still be able to stage a general uprising, a rebellion that was in no way attributable to the US but one that would quickly dislodge Fidel Castro.

The new plan was presented to Eisenhower and the Chiefs of Staff on 29 November. Neither Ike nor his advisors made any objections and by the New Year of 1961, as Eisenhower bowed out of the White House, the change of plan had been agreed.

As part of their 1960 election campaigns, both Kennedy and Richard Nixon, the two candidates for the presidency, had made great play of the threat that Castro represented. Both men took a hard line, Nixon telling Allen Dulles that the planned operation was taking far too long to come to fruition. Ideally, he had wanted Castro dealt with by the time of the election. It was not to be.

When the votes were counted Kennedy won one of the closest presidential elections in American history, a near-run thing indeed. He was inaugurated as president on 20 January 1961. On 28 January, just a week later, he was briefed by the CIA on the latest developments in various American projects across the globe. In particular there was the thorny issue of Cuba.

As president-elect, Kennedy had already had an initial discussion with Allen Dulles and Richard Bissell at Palm Beach on 18 November the previous year. And Cuba had been at the top of the agenda for all three men.

Dulles later went on record stating that this November meeting was the first JFK had heard about the proposed Cuban operation. Richard Nixon, however, was convinced that Dulles had informed his opponent about the planned invasion long before the election and that Kennedy had used the knowledge in his campaign. Dulles was rewarded by being asked to stay on as Director of the CIA even though he was long past retirement age.

Regardless of whether or not Kennedy knew about the proposals, it was at the November meeting that Bissell told him the CIA had abandoned its planned guerrilla campaign and was now in the process of putting together an assault force of Cuban exiles to make a traditional attack.

JFK and Nixon, shown here during one of their increasingly hostile TV debates during the presidential election of 1960.

There has been speculation that Dulles, and Bissell in particular, were deliberately misleading the president, knowing that no matter how much he disliked the idea, in order to make the invasion a success US forces would be required. Eisenhower had put nothing on paper about the change of plan but he certainly knew about the invasion and, having himself led a seaborne invasion during the Second World War, was more than happy to agree to the alteration. Kennedy was more doubtful.

The intention had always been to install a provisional Cuban government. This government would then request US aid once Brigade 2506 had established its beachhead. Until then US involvement had to be kept hidden. So, for the moment, Kennedy was informed only about the proposed invasion by the Cuban exiles.

In March 1961 the CIA was instrumental in creating the Cuban Revolutionary Council. This was as a direct result of President Kennedy demanding a more liberal and representative exile organization. After much debate and argument among the Cuban representatives, José Miro Cardona, the first prime minister after the toppling of Batista, was chosen to be the first chair of the new council.

Cardona had become disenchanted with the Castro regime, defected and claimed political asylum in Spain. After a brief period of refuge in the Argentinian embassy he was smuggled into the US. He now became the leader-in-waiting of the new Cuban government that was to take control once Operation Pluto, as the invasion operation was eventually named, had achieved the desired result.

José Miro Cardona, Chair of the Cuban Revolutionary Council, takes centre stage.

Operation Pluto would see 1,000 members of Brigade 2506 (the number was later increased to just under 1,500) land on the beaches around the city of Trinidad, some 200 miles to the southeast of Cuba's capital, Havana. The site for the invasion – the lodgement as it was known – was important as the city, as far as CIA intelligence was concerned, was a supposed hotbed of anti-Castro feelings. Trinidad would be a foothold in Cuban territory.

US Marine Colonel Jack Hawkins, a veteran of amphibious landings in the

Second World War and in Korea, had been brought in almost as soon as the decision was made to launch a traditional landing rather than fight a guerrilla campaign. Jacob Esterline had freely admitted that such an operation was not in his experience or skill range. Hawkins, however, had exactly the knowledge and experience needed.

In January 1961 a memo from Hawkins who was now, along with Air Force Colonel Stanley Beerli, a major player in the events that were soon to unfold, underlined the point that the landing was to be a lodgement rather than the beginning of a drive toward Havana. In other words the men of Brigade 2506 would not seek to move out from their beachhead: they would simply dig in and keep Castro's forces at bay. This, it was hoped, would provoke an uprising among the people that would achieve the desired effect of removing Castro – without the US hand being seen.

At this stage everyone seemed rather pleased with the proposals. The city of Trinidad sat close to the foothills of the Escambray Mountains which would provide cover for the Brigade should the invasion fail and the troops need to scatter. The mountains were also the home of several guerrilla groups fighting against the Castro regime.

Trinidad was a port with good docking facilities which would be useful for bringing in supplies or, if the situation demanded, for evacuation of the Brigade.

Colonel Jack Hawkins, experienced in amphibious landings and a man who was highly critical of the decision to cancel airstrikes against Castro's air force.

The seaborne invasion would be supported by aircraft and by paratroops who would be dropped inland of the port.

Kennedy tentatively approved the plan, ordering the CIA and the Chiefs of Staff to keep him informed on progress. He particularly wanted to know of any developments or changes to the existing arrangements.

Radio Swan had been operating since May 1960, the irrepressible David Phillips recording scripts in Washington before passing them to their final destination, the radio station that had been set up on Swan Island off Honduras.

The island was so insignificant that Seabees had to journey to the place to create landing facilities. Once up and running the Radio Swan broadcasts warned of coming destruction for the Castro regime along with peculiar messages such as 'Look to the rainbow' and 'The fish will rise soon'. Possibly they were intended to make Castro's officials think that Radio Swan was communicating with rebel forces on the island in the way that the BBC had sent messages to the French resistance during the Second World War.

Bizarrely, Radio Swan was both a clandestine and a commercial station, advertisements being drawn from a wide range of US businesses. Music was played and the station also carried genuine news bulletins, mixed in with considerable amounts of disinformation. Its main purpose, however, was to broadcast anti-Castro messages to the people of Cuba. Despite Castro jamming the broadcasts, the station was listened to all over the Caribbean. How effective it was remains a moot matter. Perhaps, rather like Lord Haw-Haw's broadcasts from Germany or Tokyo Rose's efforts from Japan during the Second World War, the people of Cuba viewed David Phillips's efforts more as entertainment than as news.

During his election campaign Kennedy had been so virulent in his denouncements of Castro that having now assumed power, both his administration and the American public felt he had to turn those election promises into reality. JFK knew the problem but he was not yet confident enough to take appropriate action.

General Maxwell Taylor in his later investigation of the invasion was clear that Kennedy had inherited a very difficult problem. In his opinion Kennedy's administration got the short end of the stick: 'the planned anti-Castro operation was a burr under its saddle'.

By now Fidel Castro was convinced that Cuba was about to be invaded by US forces. The furore and rhetoric flung about by both parties in the recent US election campaign could not fail to make him think otherwise. As part of the Cuban defence programme, on 30 October 1960 Castro constituted the National Revolutionary Militia, a body of willing recruits who would be trained in the use of firearms, ready to take their part in the Cuban Revolutionary Armed Forces to defend Cuba from assaults by foreign aggressors.

The new Revolutionary Militia was joined with the University Militia and, together, added 200,000 willing but not particularly well trained recruits to Castro's army. If they were not exactly Dad's Army, they were certainly defined more by enthusiasm than by military skill. These were the part-time soldiers who would bear the brunt of the fighting in case of an invasion.

It was now just a case of finding out when such an invasion was likely to take place. Castro's G2 spy network was very efficient, not only within Cuba but also in the US and across the wider Caribbean. His informants in Latin America and in Miami were able to confirm the rumours that Cuban exiles were being recruited in the US and trained in Guatemala. It was clear that something significant was about to happen in the very near future. In the meantime – keep watching.

A worried Castro felt that he could not afford to take chances. In October 1960 as the US election campaign moved towards its climax and the newly constituted militia became a reality, he placed his troops on high alert. Earthworks and trenches were dug along the coast and patrols stepped up. The Cuban people were as ready as they could be to repel any assault.

Cuban militia in training.

For once Castro had got it wrong. There was no invasion, not yet at least, but tension remained high with both Castro and the Kennedy administration feeling like they were sitting on tubs of gunpowder.

All it needed was a light for the fuse. That came in January 1961 when Castro expelled a large number of diplomats and officials from the US embassy in Havana. As almost one of his last acts as president, Eisenhower retaliated by expelling a number of Cuban officials from Washington – tit for tat indeed. The resultant severing of diplomatic relations between the two countries was made inevitable and in the days before he handed over to the new administration Eisenhower saw this particular piece of political dynamite become reality.

As far as the US government was concerned something had to be done about Castro. For a brief moment a US invasion was considered but, eventually, it was decided that things should stand as they were. Operation Pluto would go ahead.

Two presidents, Ike and JFK.

4. FINAL PLANNING

'We have made a covenant with death and with Hell we are at agreement.'

Isiah 28:15

With José Miro Cardona installed as de facto president and Dr Manuel Artime happily ensconced as the political head of the operation, it was time to look to the more practical side of the affair, the military leadership.

Head of Brigade 2506 was former Cuban army officer José 'Pepe' Perez San Román. He had undergone US officer training at Fort Benning in Georgia and had served for a while in Castro's army before being imprisoned for helping former Batista army officers to escape from Cuba.

Exiled to the US, San Román was efficient and energetic but like many others had convinced himself that the lodgement of Brigade 2506 on the Cuban beaches

was just the start of a process. American forces would back up the initial strike: 'An important psychological factor boosted the invaders' morale ... It had been repeated over and over again since they had been recruited: "The Americans are with us, and the Americans can't lose."'

Pepe San Román's second in command and, like him, a man who would soon face the shells and bullets on the invasion beaches, was Erneido Oliva Gonzalez. He was also a former Cuban army officer, an experienced soldier who had been forced out of Cuba by Castro in 1960.

Despite the appointment of these experienced and capable leaders, backed up, in the main, by effective battalion commanders, there remained a simple but fundamental weakness in the invasion force: the men who had been enlisted to carry out the operation.

Pepe San Román, Brigade leader, shown here in prison after the invasion.

There was nothing wrong with their hearts or their intentions but once the decision had been made to abandon guerrilla tactics, Brigade 2506 was forced to expand from just over 500 men to 1,500 in a relatively short space of time. It was neither as easy to find potentially good soldiers as previously nor as easy to train them. Putting a gun in a man's hands and telling him to go and invade Cuba was far from the answer to the problem.

Only 135 of the expanded Brigade were former soldiers, the rest being students (240 of them), fishermen, peasants and a strange conglomeration of doctors, lawyers and businessmen. They were willing and brave but no matter how much training they were given in the few weeks available, they were still amateurs.

Arthur Schlesinger Jr, perhaps the most perceptive of all Kennedy's advisors, later wrote that although the spirit of the men was high there were serious issues: 'Many of the new recruits had been at the base for only a few days. Some had not even fired a gun.'

After November 1960 the Brigade was organized into seven battalions, each of which was broken down into companies, platoons and nine-man squads. They were armed with Garand and Johnson rifles and M-1A1 carbines, bayonets and hand grenades. Each company was also equipped with mortars, recoilless guns, flame throwers and bazookas. In addition there were trucks armed with machine guns, jeeps and even a bulldozer.

A tank unit consisting of five M-41 Walker Bulldog medium tanks was also made available to the Brigade. Unfortunately, the plan was

Fidel Castro doing what he always did best – courting publicity. He is shown here with the writer Ernest Hemingway who, for a time, lived on Cuba, and who too was not averse to public exposure.

45

for these tanks to operate as infantry support, not as a regular armoured unit, and consequently when the landing was made they were spread across the whole invasion area. This was eventually a distance of over twenty miles, meaning that the tanks could have only limited effect as offensive weapons.

Air support consisted, initially, of ten Second World War-vintage B-26 Invaders and a number of Curtiss C-46 Commandos for transport duties. Ex-Navy Douglas A-1 Skyraiders were offered and seriously considered by the CIA but were eventually rejected as there were no similar planes operating in the region and their sudden appearance in the skies over Latin America would derail the American claim of plausible deniability.

The Brigade air force, Fuerza Aerea de Liberación or the FAL (as opposed to Castro's air force, the Fuerza Aerea de Revolución or the FAR) was under the overall command of Colonel Manuel Villafana. Training and leadership at the 'coal face' came from American pilots and agents.

A number of other aircraft were acquired as training went on. These included a Consolidated PBY Catalina and a Lockheed L-1649 Starliner Constellation. Extra B-26s were also added to the force, many of them being cannibalized for parts and equipment. Eventually the Brigade was supplied with sixteen B-26 bombers and six C-54 transports.

With training aircraft being different in performance and handling techniques from the eventual operational aircraft, progress was slow and there was not yet any real appreciation of what would later become common knowledge, as the CIA later revealed: 'What happened in the air not only could, but did, determine the fate of the US government's anti-Castro program.'

Importantly, no fighter cover would be available. The short range of any fighters the Brigade might obtain meant that they could only operate out of the US and that would openly advertise US involvement. Yet again the concept of plausible deniability would have a detrimental effect on the planned invasion.

As there was to be no fighter cover, the CIA requested that the B-26s come with the standard armament of eight 12.7mm machine guns in the nose. Castro's FAR also operated B-26 bombers but with a significant difference. Their noses were made from Plexiglas and consequently their guns were mounted in the wings rather than the nose. In the days ahead this was to become an important distinction.

Training of the small unit of paratroops was carried out at a Guatemalan base near St José airfield. The paratroopers quickly christened the base 'Garrapatenango' because of the numerous bugs or ticks in the area (*garrapatas* are ticks). Nevertheless, they carried on quite happily with their training, making numerous practice drops each week.

With the decision to launch a seaborne invasion rather than guerrilla attacks there was an urgent need for ships. In keeping with the concept of plausible deniability, the US State Department had insisted that no American ships should be involved and so the CIA turned to private enterprise.

The Garcia Line, a small shipping company, was one of the few Cuban lines still operating out of Miami. Five of their out-of-date, virtually redundant 2,000-ton freighters were leased to the CIA for $600 a day, plus expenses.

The company owner, Eduardo Garcia, was told what his ships would be expected to do but was also informed that they would have US air cover and that, therefore, there was little risk. The first four vessels, *Atlántico*, *Caribe*, *Houston* and *Rio Escondido* would carry supplies and weapons to the beachhead while the *Lake Charles* was earmarked to transport the new Cuban government to the island.

The ships were also to carry thirty-six aluminium motorboats powered by outboard motors plus a number of inflatables. Out of their mothball fleet, the US Navy made available two Landing Craft (Infantry), the *Blagar* and the *Barbara J*, both of which were Second World War vintage but which had been extensively reconditioned to act as heavily armed escort vessels and command ships. Three Landing Craft (Utilities) and four Landing Craft (Vehicles and Personnel) made up the rest of the fleet.

The Garcia Line ships would be crewed by merchant navy sailors who were used to handling cargo vessels of this type but not necessarily in combat zones. The landing craft were run by US Navy personnel but, importantly, not by sailors with combat experience. These were men skilled in logistics and supply but not experienced in working under enemy fire.

At first glance Brigade 2506 seemed well equipped and well organized. But there were significant cracks in the arrangements. With Cuban officers leading the attacks 'on the ground' and Americans taking nominal but distant control, there were always going to be communication difficulties.

Many of the Cubans felt that American involvement at the operational level did more harm than good and the FRD was clear – control of the invasion should not be in the hands of foreigners, however friendly they might be. It was the FRD, they felt, that should appoint brigade and battalion commanders, not Americans.

Colonel Jack Hawkins was well aware of the problem. He was, later, quite specific in his understanding where blame for the failure of the scheme lay: 'Divided command and responsibility at the operational level was not in keeping with standard military procedure.'

Once again plausible deniability was a governing factor with US officials wanting to maintain their involvement but not being willing to stand up and be counted.

The harbour at Playa Larga. (Photo Kaldari)

In November 1960 when the decision was made to move from a guerrilla operation to a standard military assault the whole idea of plausible deniability was no longer realistic. Eisenhower and then Kennedy as the in-coming president should have been informed of this and the whole affair either abandoned or turned over to the Pentagon. But the CIA, Dulles and Bissell in particular were intent on sticking to their plan. They had already been forced into changes once; they did not want to alter things again. It was unfortunate for them that they were about to do exactly that.

On 11 March at a meeting of high-ranking officials – including Jack and Bobby Kennedy, Secretary of State Dean Rusk, Defense Secretary Robert McNamara, Milo Cardona and the Joint Chiefs of Staff – it was clear that no firm decision had yet been reached regarding the landing. To the surprise of people like Cardona it seemed as if the operation was still in a state of flux and could, even now, be called off.

Kennedy vacillated. During the meeting he seriously questioned the viability of the proposed invasion which, if US involvement was traced, would be bound to undo all the worldwide good will that had been shown to the new Kennedy administration over the past month.

Allen Dulles was not happy, arguing that the US had created Brigade 2506 and to disband it now would be detrimental to the US reputation as champion of the downtrodden. It would also create what he called a 'dispersal problem'. The thought of 1,500 disgruntled armed men roaming across Central America was not an issue that could be ignored. Kennedy finally agreed, commenting that if they had to get rid of the Brigade 'it was better to dump them in Cuba than in the United States, especially if that is where they want to go.'

The decision might have been made but JFK reserved the right to order a cancellation as late as twenty-four hours before the proposed landing date. Dulles and

Secretary of Defense
Robert McNamara.

Secretary of State
Dean Rusk.

Bissell breathed a sigh of relief. So did the Joint Chiefs of Staff who might later claim that they had no ownership of the proposed invasion but could not deny that they were kept informed and knew all about the developments. Kennedy, however, did have one other serious concern as Schlesinger recounted: 'Bissell renewed the case for the Trinidad plan. Kennedy questioned it as "too spectacular." He did not want a big amphibious invasion in the manner of the Second World War; he wanted a "quiet" landing, preferably at night.'

Historians and analysts, even the participants themselves, might deplore the decision to change the venue for the landings but with plausible deniability still governing all decision, it is hard not to see where Kennedy was coming from.

The airfield at Trinidad was too small to accommodate the B-26 bombers that were now an integral part of the plan. The aircraft would have to fly from their new base at Happy Valley in Puerto Cabezas, Nicaragua, or possibly even from Florida and that would destroy the idea of there being no US involvement in the invasion. Only aerial attacks from Cuba itself would preserve the illusion and that, inevitably, meant that a Trinidad landing was out.

Trinidad was also heavily populated and by its nature quite a conspicuous port. Plausible deniability could only work in a clandestine way and the very openness of Trinidad made this, Kennedy felt, more or less impossible. As Commander-in-Chief, with the power to overrule even the Joint Chiefs of Staff, his view had to be acknowledged.

Over the next three days CIA planners considered alternative landing sites. There were two or three possibilities but the most likely, they decided, lay approximately

Richard Bissell, a man with ambitions that were doomed never to reach fruition.

100 miles west of Trinidad in the area the Americans called the Bay of Pigs, the Cubans Bahia de Cochinos.

There was little in the area apart from the two small towns of Girón and Larga, tree-lined strands of what appeared to be welcoming sand and, significantly, the airstrip at Playa Girón which was long enough to take the B-26 bombers. The area was remote although Castro and his government had plans to develop a holiday complex at Playa Girón. Construction work on the cottages and other accommodation was already partially complete but one of the advantages of attacking at night and on a weekend was that most of the workers would have finished for the week and gone home.

The encroaching Zapata Swamp, infested with mosquitoes and crocodiles, would offer a natural defence should the Cubans send in reinforcements. The fact that it could also trap Brigade 2506 and contain the invaders on the beaches was conveniently ignored.

The Chiefs of Staff agreed to the proposition, remarking that they would still have preferred the Trinidad option. Kennedy noted their opinions but chose to ignore them and, on 15 March 1961, duly authorized the Bay of Pigs landing.

JFK and his Joint Chiefs of Staff.

Playa Larga in the Bay of Pigs.

Three landing beaches had been chosen. Playa Larga (Red Beach) was the northernmost spot at the top end of the bay, Playa Girón (Blue Beach) lay some twenty miles to the southeast and the third site was farther east again at Caleta Buena Inlet on the road to Cienfuegos (Green Beach). The deserted nature of the beaches and hinterland should, the planners hoped, fulfil President Kennedy's desire for a 'quiet' landing. How the offloading of 1,500 men, complete with heavy equipment and support vehicles was to remain clandestine was never explained.

The CIA remained adamant that 500 guerrillas would join Brigade 2506 the moment the beachhead was established with another 5,000 to arrive within two days. Dr Cardona put the figure higher, at 10,000. It was no more than wishful thinking.

British intelligence sources clearly indicated that Cubans were unlikely to react to an invasion by rising against Castro. British ambassador David Ormsby Gore, a personal friend of JFK's, passed on the disquieting news but, in the end, the information was ignored.

The Brigade's paratroops would be dropped further inland – at Horquitas, at Jocuma close to the Cavadonga Sugar Mill and on the road connecting the Australia Sugar Mill to Playa Larga. As well as creating 'inland beachheads', their job was to close road access to the landing beaches.

The town of Trinidad, with the Escambray Mountains in the background. (Photo Trudy Carradice)

With the change of lodgement area to the Bay of Pigs, control of the skies above Cuba now became vitally important for the men of Brigade 2506. It meant that Lieutenant Colonel George Gaines as project officer for the planned invasion and Garfield Thorsrud (Gar as he was known by all and sundry) as acting chief of the air section immediately assumed positions of great power.

The change in location mattered little to the CIA planners. The intention was to strike hard and quickly at Castro's air force, knocking out aircraft while they were still on the ground. Support facilities would also be targeted.

And so, Trinidad or the Bay of Pigs? To them it hardly mattered. After much debate and changing of ideas, the air attacks came down to strikes on three Cuban airfields at Libertad, San Antonio and Santiago. Gar Thorsrud had no doubts about the success of these strikes: 'We had napalm earmarked for the tanks lined up on the soccer field. And we had .50 calibre [guns] – the 8-gun-nose B-26s, which was a hell of a lot of firepower – to hit the parked aircraft. There was just no doubt in anyone's mind that, with the element of surprise, at the crack of dawn that first day, that there wouldn't have been anything left on any of those fields.'

The key, of course, was that element of surprise. There was no doubt that Castro's G2 had told him how close the CIA now was to launching an attack. He seemed to have a sixth sense where danger was concerned, a skill that had served him well during his long years as a guerrilla fighter in the Escambray Mountains.

Kennedy commented that Castro did not require an intelligence service to keep him informed this time. If he wanted news or information he simply had to read the American newspapers which were full of articles about the Brigade and its intentions.

How best to achieve the surprise attacks was one of the constant debates or discussions in the final days before the invasion was launched. National Security Advisor McGeorge Bundy put the matter quite succinctly: 'The revised landing plan depends strongly upon prompt action against Castro's air [force]. The question in my mind is whether we cannot solve the problem by having the airstrike some little time before the invasion.'

This quickly became the plan. Airstrikes would be launched at dawn and dusk on D-2 (15 April) with an option for similar attacks on D-1. At dawn on D-Day, Monday 17 April, the FAL would go in again, just prior to the landings.

That, at least, was the intention but as things turned out, cancellation of the afternoon strike on the 15th and both proposed strikes on the 16th – decisions made by the Kennedy administration rather than the CIA or military planners – halted all but the initial attack. It was a puzzling decision – one that was kept

National Security Advisor
McGeorge Bundy.

from Brigade 2506 until the last moment – as whoever controlled the air over Cuba controlled the whole operation.

Still obsessed with plausible deniability, the aircraft of Brigade 2506 were painted in Cuban colours and given FAR markings. The intention was to hide their real identity and, once again, prevent any possibility of the US being inculpated.

As far as the world was concerned, these attacking planes were Cuban aircraft flown by FAR pilots who had become dissatisfied with the Castro regime. Disguising aircraft in this manner was against the terms of the Geneva Convention but nobody seemed to care too much.

The lack of clear markings on the FAL and FAR planes would remain a problem throughout the campaign. There were several instances of 'friendly fire' and in one case toward the end of the operation severe damage was sustained by a Cuban militia convoy after an attack by their own FAR aircraft.

A number of infiltrators – the last kick of the original plan – were to be dropped inland in the area beyond the Zapata Swamp. Their purpose was to blow bridges, power stations, roads and other strategic sites and link up with existing Cuban guerrilla groups. Above all they were to cause as much confusion as possible.

Several of the CIA planners still harboured a hope that the Brigade might eventually break out and link up with its own infiltrators and the guerrilla fighters

Coastal Cuba: little has changed. (Photo Trudy Carradice)

in the Escambray Mountains. It was wishful thinking of the highest order. The route to the mountains, which lay some sixty or seventy miles away from the Zapata Peninsula, was across enemy-held territory and open to constant attack from both air and land. Hindsight it may well have been but later CIA analysis of the idea was both sceptical and scathing: 'Reference to even the most simplistic topographic map would have quickly ended all such speculation.'

And so for the men of Brigade 2506 the witching hour inched precariously closer. They had been trained and equipped. Now, at last, it was time to take back Cuba and destroy the influence, once and for all, of Fidel Castro.

5. ATTACK

> 'Cry havoc, and unleash the dogs of war.'
>
> Shakespeare, *Julius Caesar*

Operation Puma, the first aerial assault on Castro's Cuba, took place early on the morning of 15 April 1961. Richard Bissell, reacting to the concerns of President Kennedy, had become increasingly worried that large-scale aerial attacks would incriminate the US and, contrary to the original idea, he ordered a significant reduction in the number of aircraft involved. Like so many other bad calls during the operation it was a fatal move.

The original idea had been for intensive attacks to be made against the Cuban airfields where FAR planes were stationed with the intention of destroying the FAR on the ground. As a plan it was insightful and realistic, ensuring that the Cuban air force would not be able to interfere in any way with the landings.

Full-scale assault or reduced-strength attacks? Before anything could be done the first stage was to ascertain the number of FAR planes stationed at each of the Cuban airfields. U2 reconnaissance sorties on 11 and 13 April indicated that at

U2 reconnaissance aircraft were used to take photographs of the Cuban airfields after the initial airstrike.

Campo Libertad five B-26s and five Sea Furies were stationed. At San Antonio de los Banos were five B-26s, one Lockheed T-33 Shooting Star and one Sea Fury. The airfield at Santiago, which did not normally play host to FAR planes, held two B-26s, one T-33 and a derelict Sea Fury.

The number of B-26 bombers was the first major concern. Apart from the location and number of their guns the B-26s of the FAR were basically the same as those flown by the FAL. Durable but slow the B-26 had been the workhorse of many a campaign over the years and this, for the aerial forces of both sides, was to be more or less its last fling.

The T-33s, whose power and manoeuvrability were to be constantly undervalued by the Brigade during the invasion, had at this stage of their active service life been relegated to what was essentially the role of jet trainers. However, the Cubans had added a number of 50-calibre machine guns to each plane, making them a highly effective response to the Brigade's B-26s.

The Sea Fury was a British-made fighter, a little outdated but still effective in the hands of an experienced pilot. It was a descendant of the Hawker Hurricane of Battle of Britain fame and like the earlier plane was loved by the men who flew it.

It was essential to know where these aircraft were located and unfortunately for the FAL the US reconnaissance mission got it wrong. Low cloud and a partial

For the ordinary people of Cuba, Castro was a saviour. (Photo Theodore Hensolt)

haze hindered photography of San Antonio de los Banos where there were actually three T-33s, four Sea Furies, three B-26s, three C-47s and a number of smaller aircraft on the base.

In addition, Fidel Castro, realizing that an invasion was close, had ordered his air force to take evasive action – in other words to relocate or camouflage their 'best' aircraft, leaving mainly out-of-date or damaged planes on open view.

All in all it meant that the Cuban FAR was in possession of 36 functioning combat aircraft, perhaps double the number that US reconnaissance indicated. Against this considerable force, Bissell's new plan was to launch just eight B-26 bombers to destroy the three Cuban airfields and their aircraft.

In addition to the eight attacking aircraft the Brigade had one spare or auxiliary plane to fill in if the situation demanded. As it happened this extra aircraft took no part in the operation as engine failure meant that it did not even leave the runway at Happy Valley.

A tenth aircraft had a different mission. Mario Zuniga took off from Happy Valley at 4 a.m. just after the attacking squadrons had departed for the Cuban airfields. Flying at 300 feet above Cuba, he swung west and headed for Miami. He dropped his bombs into the sea and, as the Florida coast came into view, feathered one of his engines and radioed a May Day distress signal. He landed at Miami International Airport at 8.21 am and, wearing a Cuban-made T shirt and baseball cap, was taken into custody by the US Immigration Service. The Immigration Service was gentle with him, probably having been tipped off by the CIA.

When his aircraft was examined it was found to have bullet holes in its fuselage and engine cowling. This supported Zuniga's claim that he had defected from the FAR and flown to Libertad where he and two other 'defectors' had bombed the airfield. He then returned to his own base at San Antonio, he said, attacked it and made for the US to claim political asylum. His pilot's log, sweet wrappers and receipts in the cockpit seemed to back up his claim. In fact Zuniga's mission was part of a CIA deception designed to reinforce the notion that the US was not involved in the air attacks. The bullet holes were not Cuban – but as Richard Burton was later to say in one of his films, 'What the hell, a hole is a hole is a hole.' These bullet holes had been made by the FAL, aided, advised and guided by the CIA.

Unfortunately the deception plan was itself as full of holes as a leaking colander or, as Jim Rasenberger put it 'as the cowling on Zuniga's plane'. To begin with the story was believed implicitly. The news was broadcast on TV and radio and, at the request of Cuban Foreign Minister Raúl Rosa, on the evening of 15 April an emergency session of the UN Security Council was called.

After previous discussions with Bissell's deputy, the smooth-talking and urbane Tracy Barnes, Adlai Stevenson made an impassioned reply to Rosa's charge of

American involvement in the aerial attacks. He denied any US involvement and repeated the story that the attacks on Cuban airfields had been carried out by Cuban defectors.

As far as the deception ploy was concerned, Stevenson even produced photographic evidence, sent through from Miami that morning, to show that Zuniga's story was perfectly true. At this stage Adlai Stevenson had been completely taken in. He neither knew nor understood about the CIA deception and did not for one minute think that he would be lied to by his own government.

Meanwhile, even as Zuniga sat in front of the immigration officers recounting his false cover story, the aerial attacks on Cuban airfields were proceeding. After take-off the planes immediately divided into three escadrilles or flights. Escadrille Gorilla under the command of Captain Gustavo Ponza consisted of two aircraft, Escadrille Puma (Captain José Crespo) three and Escadrille Linda, led by Captain Luis Cosme, also with three.

The planes of Escadrille Gorilla were first to arrive over their target. A Cuban patrol boat had reported their approach as soon as they entered Cuban air

Adlai Stevenson, distraught after he learned that the message he had given to the United Nations – no US involvement in the invasion – was false.

The result of the first bombing mission against Santiago.

space but they flew on and a few minutes before 6 a.m. they began their attack on Santiago. Guns, rockets and bombs were used, the pilots claiming to have destroyed AA batteries and damaged the runway as well as taking out a number of aircraft. A fuel depot was also hit before the B-26s ran out of ammunition and were forced to return to Happy Valley.

Escadrille Puma attacked Ciudad Libertad which, contrary to belief, had only a limited number of FAR planes. As the headquarters base of the FAR, however, Libertad had been equipped with extensive anti-aircraft weapons and this was to be an important factor in the assault. Vehicles and equipment, including some AA guns, were destroyed but two of the attacking aircraft were hit and seriously damaged by anti-aircraft fire from the ground.

One of the damaged B-26s managed to limp to Key West at the southernmost tip of Florida where it crash-landed on the runway of the naval base. But for the second aircraft, hit as it made a third pass over Libertad, there was no such luck. With smoke pouring out of its engine, the plane managed to stagger out of AA range but then exploded and crashed into the sea off the Cuban coast. Pilot Fernandez Mon and his navigator Gaston Perez became the first members of Brigade 2506 to die in combat.

The third attack that morning was by Escadrille Linda on San Antonio de los Banos. According to the aircrews, a number of aircraft were destroyed on the ground despite heavy defensive fire. Two of the planes then headed back to Happy Valley but the third, which had developed fuel problems, was forced to make an emergency landing on the British Grand Cayman Island. The crew were soon transferred, first to the US and then to Nicaragua and, in due course, American ground crews recovered the aircraft.

Castro's T-33s and Sea Furies might have been old – the Sea Furies propeller driven – but they were a lot faster and more effective than the Brigade's lumbering B-26-s. In a one-to-one encounter there was no doubt which side would come off best but on 15 April the FAR pilots were caught with their trousers down – in one case quite literally.

In the face of the bombing and strafing attacks, some of the Cuban pilots managed to scramble their aircraft, Gustavo Bourzac wearing only his underwear, for example. No matter how fast their planes, by the time they were in the air the FAL aircraft were already halfway back to Nicaragua. Bourzac flew as far as Key West, fruitlessly searching for the enemy before returning to base. Excitement gone, modesty set in and after landing he refused to leave his cockpit until someone brought out his clothing.

As the FAL aircraft swept low over Happy Valley Gar Thorsrud waited anxiously to see how many of his charges had made it back and how well they had done. Despite their losses, the aircrews were jubilant, the pilots convinced that they had destroyed all their targets.

The CIA, after collecting the combat reports, estimated that 80 per cent of Castro's air force had been disabled in the early morning attacks. Such a figure was hopelessly optimistic but if it had been accurate it would have meant that with the invasion only two days away the FAR would not have had time to repair or replace damaged aircraft. If the claims were true they would have only five or six functioning aircraft on D-Day.

From the early days of aerial warfare bomber pilots had always exaggerated their successes. It was difficult to be objective with cannon shells and machine-gun bullets flying everywhere and so a U2 reconnaissance plane was dispatched to take photographs that would confirm the success of the assaults. The FAL pilots waited anxiously for the results.

Eight Cubans had been killed in the attacks; many more had been wounded and Fidel Castro made great political mileage out of the incident. An official state funeral was immediately organized for the next day, thousands turning up to mourn and pay their respects to the dead heroes of the revolution.

Fidel also made great play out of the story of Eduardo Garcia Delgado, a young militia soldier mortally wounded at Libertad. Aware that he was dying, he managed to crawl to the door of his hut and, using his own blood, scrawl the word 'Fidel' onto the woodwork. True or apocryphal, Fidel made a point of taking the press to the base and gleefully showing them the young man's final word of defiance.

If Castro was enjoying something of a field day, for the CIA and the airmen of the FAL the situation now began to turn unpleasant. The U2 photographs showed that the pilots had been over-optimistic in their claims with the hit ratio on Castro's planes nowhere near the 80 per cent claimed by the FAL. No significant damage had been inflicted on the airfields either, as later reported by the CIA: 'The overflights the next day ... showed only five aircraft definitely destroyed. And not all of the attacking planes made it back to the base.'

Castro's tactic of disguising his aircraft and moving them to safe areas of each airbase had been largely successful. The planes that the FAL pilots had claimed as destroyed were, in most cases, old machines that were either out of service or in the process of being repaired.

And then there was the issue of Mario Zuniga and his deception flight. Initially successful, the lie soon turned sour when an astute reporter noticed protecting tape stretched over the barrels of the B-26 guns. Tape such as this, everyone knew, was often used as a cover to keep dust out of the gun barrels. How could the tape have remained in place, the reporter asked, if the guns had been fired, as Zuniga had claimed? There was also a significant discrepancy in Zuniga's flight log. A missing two hours between the two supposed attacks on Libertad and San Antonio could not be explained away. Most telling of all was the nose of the B-26 which was now resting quietly at Miami airport. It was made of solid metal and housed the eight guns that the CIA had requested at the beginning of the operation. Castro's FAR machines were equipped with a Plexiglas nose, their forward-firing guns being hidden in the wings. This was not an FAR plane and clearly Zuniga's flight was a set-up.

When the news was passed to Adlai Stevenson in New York he was furious. Having made what amounted to a false statement to the world, he felt betrayed by the CIA and by Kennedy's administration. For a while, he seriously considered resigning his position as US Ambassador to the United Nations. It took all Kennedy's persuasive powers to get him to stay.

The failed deception ploy and the unimpressive airstrikes had several significant results, all of them very far from the intended effects. Firstly, rather than dishearten the Cuban people, the airstrikes united them behind their leader in a way that nothing had yet done. If he had been popular before, now Castro was a hero. Colonel George Gaines, project officer for the invasion summed it up precisely and succinctly: 'From Castro to common labourers the D-2 airstrike got the Cubans together.'

Domingo Rodriguez, a fisherman from the town of Girón, was a young boy at the time. For him it was not just getting behind Fidel Castro; the Bay of Pigs attack – all of it, airstrikes and invasion – was a much more seismic event. It literally changed his life. In a 2011 interview with the BBC World Service he described his feelings both during the invasion scare and afterwards: 'It was like a great school for the Cuban people; we finally learned that we don't have to be afraid of the enemy.'

For Cubans in 1961 there could only be one possible enemy: the United States of America. If Fidel was suddenly the most popular hero of the nation, John F. Kennedy was the devil incarnate.

The airstrikes also alerted Castro and his government to the impending invasion. They had been expecting it for months; now they knew it was coming within the next few days. Early airstrikes were a risk worth taking – as long as they were successful. The attacks on D-2 were disastrous, thereby defeating the whole purpose of the exercise.

In the wake of the attacks the remaining FAR aircraft were dispersed to the fringes of the airbases, suitably disguised and protected. The pilots were ordered to sleep beneath the wings of their aircraft, ready for an immediate scramble.

Castro also ordered the arrest and detention of anyone who might conceivably be tempted to take up arms to assist the invading troops. Some sources say as many as half a million people were taken into custody, others place the figure at 200,000. Either way, it was an enormous number and any faint hopes of a popular rising to assist Brigade 2506 vanished at that moment.

Most important of all, American duplicity and Adlai Stevenson's anger at being given deliberately erroneous information led directly to the cancelling of the second D-2 strike. That, on its own, was not the end of the world. But Kennedy went one stage further and, acting on the advice of Secretary of State Dean Rusk, also cancelled all the potential attacks on D-1 and the planned attacks on Cuban airfields on D-Day itself.

The decision was made because Kennedy and Rusk firmly believed that a second and third strike would place the US in an untenable position as the aggressor. Only if planes could fly from Cuba, or at least *appear* to fly from Cuba, would another airstrike against Castro's FAR take place. The B-26s would be used on D Day but only to protect the infantry landings.

It was a crucial decision that meant the operation was, ultimately, bound to fail. With strikes against Castro's airfields ruled out, the FAR still had the aerial power

Cuba during the 1940s and 1950s was a mob-funded tourist paradise – music, food, wine and women aplenty.

Above: Brigade 2506 flag.

Below left: CIA seal.

Below right: Brigade 2506 shield.

Above: The town of Trindad – mooted as a possible Brigade 2506 beachhead – in the lee of the Escambray Mountains. (Photo Trudy Carradice)

Below: Havana's waterfront. (Photo Yeoztudioz)

B-26 light attack bombers in action in this machismo-inspired US Army Air Forces recruiting poster.

A Cuban Sea Fury at the Girón museum. (Photo Alexandra)

A Douglas Invader with false Cuban air force markings at the Wings over Miami museum, Tamiami airport. (Photo RuthAS)

Above: A tropical paradise, Playa Girón today, Blue Beach of the invasion. (Photo Gorupdebesanez)

Below: An immaculately maintained Cuban T-34 at the Girón museum (Photo anagoria)

Above left: Fidel, the master propagandist, as he would like to be remembered.

Above right: A Cuban stamp issued to commemorate the invasion.

Below: A billboard at Playa Girón proclaims: "*Aqui se libro un combate decisivo para la victoria*", roughly translated as "Here you can book a decisive fight for victory". (Photo Steph32)

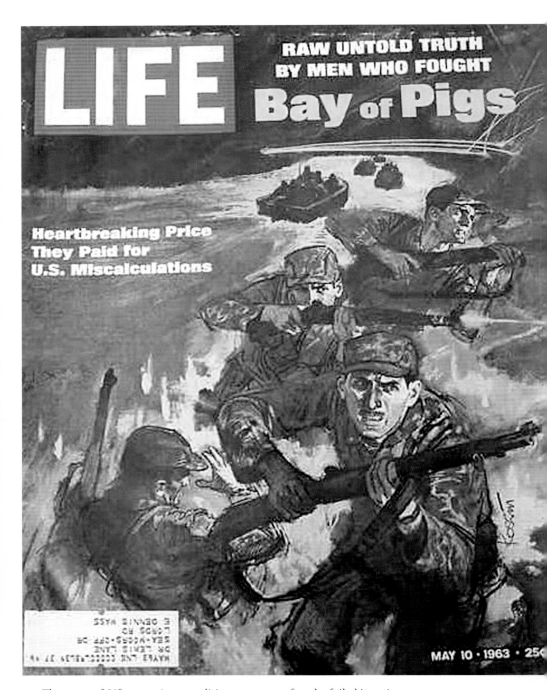

The cover of *Life* magazine, an edition two years after the failed invasion.

to attack and seriously maul the invading Brigade. The FAL planes coming from Happy Valley in Nicaragua – several hours' flying time away from Cuba – did not have the fuel capacity to spend more than very short periods of time over the beaches.

Leaving Castro's air force more or less intact also meant that the Brigade aircraft, as they attempted to provide ground support to the troops on the beaches, would be exposed to the enemy T-33 and Sea Fury fighters. It was, quite literally, a no-win situation, as many people appreciated, not least the CIA in a later report: 'In the most simplistic of terms, the US government's anti-Castro program which climaxed at the Bay of Pigs might have succeeded only if the air operations as evolved by the CIA had been retained intact.'

Cartoon showing JFK with his cigar blowing up in his face – an apt analogy.

More significantly, the cancellations adversely affected the most important part of the whole invasion plan, the capture and use of Girón airfield. As Kennedy had so often said, the only way he would allow further aerial attacks on Castro's FAR was if Brigade aircraft were to fly off Cuban soil. The first part of the plan had been completed but use of the field simply did not happen. Lynch: 'The vehicles, the tanks, the fuel tanker truck, and the armaments for the B-26s were in position at the airfield. Everything was set to rearm and refuel the Brigade planes but, with Castro's jets in the air, none of our planes dared to land.'

Girón airfield remained unused, apart from one brief supply drop under the cover of darkness. And even then the pilot was adamant that he had to be away before sun-up. It was yet another nail in the coffin of the Brigade, yet another chance missed.

The blame for what was seen as a dramatic mistake has to remain with Kennedy. It was a move that none of the military men had expected. General Curtis LeMay was standing in for Air Force Chief of Staff General Thomas White at a meeting on 16 April. When he was told of the decision LeMay, never the most understated of individuals, was appalled:

'You just cut everybody's throats down there,' LeMay told Under Secretary of Defense Roswell Gilpatric.

'What do you mean?' Gilpatric asked.

LeMay explained that without air support, the land forces were doomed. Gilpatric simply shrugged.

The shrug may or may not have been significant. Either way, cancelling the air-strikes was a clear case of a politician, obsessed with the idea of plausible denia-bility, overriding military opinion. America's hand must not be seen in any of the dirty dealings that typified the Bay of Pigs affair. And, of course, it led to wrong decisions being made. The military men were upset and even some of the politi-cians in Washington questioned Kennedy's decision as later reported by the CIA: 'The last minute cancellation of the D Day strike was clearly a case where profes-sional military judgement was negated by political expediency.'

For the FAL pilots, Happy Valley suddenly seemed a long way from the action. The cancellation of the second D-2 raids came first. The pilots accepted it as a routine circumstance of war, believing that men like Colonel Stanley Beerli and Gar Thorsrud would not let them down. They could wait until the early morning strikes of the next day.

Several of the pilots were actually sitting in their cockpits waiting to take off

for that dawn raid when the cancella-tion order came through. In the com-mand hut, Gar Thorsrud received and read the cable from Beerli and could not believe his eyes. But he was a good soldier and reluctantly complied with the order. Then he went outside to console his men. It was a devastat-ing blow that blighted the morale of the FAL pilots. They had trained for this for months and now, as they saw it, they were being side-lined for rea-sons that nobody could understand or appreciate.

The FAL had been left with twelve aircraft after the operations of 15 April. One of their B-26 bombers had been destroyed, another three were out of action in Florida or on the Grand Cayman. But the pilots were still willing to carry on – if they were given the chance.

General Curtis LeMay, outspoken critic of the decision to suspend bombing missions against Castro's airfields and aircraft.

For JFK, keeping the US out of the spotlight was everything and it led to decisions being made that should not have been made. If ever there was a disastrous concept that destroyed lives and dreams it was plausible deniability, an idea that was now being shown as a non-starter.

Kennedy was later to bemoan the fact that he had placed his brother Bobby in the Justice Department where he was 'wasted'. He should, Kennedy said, have had a more active role in the running of the government, in particular the CIA. (In the months ahead Bobby Kennedy duly became one of JFK's principal advisors, regardless of his position as Attorney General. That was only after the Bay of Pigs affair was over and by then, of course, for the men on the Cuban beaches it was already too late. Bobby Kennedy's influence, undoubtedly for good, during the forthcoming Cuban Missile Crisis was immense, leaving historians and the public to wonder what might have happened had he been more fully involved in April 1961.)

It was not just JFK who was at fault over the aerial attacks. The CIA had to shoulder at least some of the blame, the whole operation having been planned by Bissell and his team. They were undoubtedly aware of the importance of air cover but now, faced by an adamant and unbending presidential attitude, they meekly gave in. It was a strange about-face and the later internal CIA investigation into the Bay of Pigs disaster commented: 'Senior Agency personnel were negligent in failing to recognize that there was a point beyond which they should no longer have tolerated political interference with the planned military operation.'

It was an astute comment, clearly aimed at Richard Bissell. The leader of the operation, along with General Cabell, deputy to Allen Dulles, later came in for direct criticism when the official CIA history of the invasion took them to task for not pressing their case with sufficient force.

That same negligence and lack of dynamic opposition was also apparent in the reactions of the Joint Chiefs of Staff when they heard the news. Jack Hawkins immediately telephoned General David Shoup, commandant of the US Marine Corps, pleading for him get Kennedy to change his mind. He was met with a bland refusal. Shoup reminded Hawkins that the president had made his decision. Perhaps Shoup was right not to approach Kennedy but as someone with extensive experience in amphibious landings he should have at least tried. Kennedy might have been prepared to take that experience into consideration and, at the very least, listen to him.

When he was told later that night, General Lyman Lemnitzer, chair of the Joint Chiefs of Staff, called the decision 'almost criminal'. And yet, like Shoup, he did not attempt to telephone the president and express his disapproval. Lemnitzer's sole concession or nod to history was to approve the request of Charles Cabell for naval air cover. Of course, he told the deputy director of the CIA, the president

Che, a man of the people.

would have to be informed the following morning and approve that decision before anything could be done. And everyone knew that no such approval would be forthcoming.

Cabell himself could have contacted the president. He did not. Whether a telephone call from such an experienced man as Cabell, or for that matter from people like Shoup and Lemnitzer, would have caused Kennedy to change his mind remains an imponderable. What was – and is – quite clear is that nobody even attempted to stand up to JFK, thereby condemning the Bay of Pigs invasion to defeat and disaster.

For those, like Colonel Jack Hawkins, who understood the significance of air power it was a galling and frustrating time: 'all of Castro's fighters must be destroyed on the ground prior to the landings. If only one of his fighters is left intact, the invasion forces must withdraw at once, otherwise this operation will result in complete disaster.'

Whatever reason intelligent and experienced men had for failing to use their initiative or fight their corner, it was clear on that fateful Saturday night that there would be no more airstrikes against Castro's bases, neither on D-1 nor on D-Day itself. Brigade 2506 was on its own.

6. INVASION

'People will continue to commit atrocities as long as they believe in absurdities.'

Voltaire

During the morning and afternoon of 13 April the men of Brigade 2506 were moved from Trax Base to Puerto Cabezas in Nicaragua, the departure point for the invasion force. Equipment and supplies had been loaded onto the waiting freighters the previous day while heavy vehicles like trucks and tanks were safely stored on board the US landing ship *San Marco*.

The *San Marco*, in company with the aircraft carrier *Essex* and the escorting destroyers that made up US Navy Task Force Alpha, was already at sea. Hull numbers on the US ships had been painted out but the flotilla had orders to remain outside Cuban territorial waters. There was to be no contact, unless it originated from the Cuban forces. The job of Task Force Alpha was purely to support, from a distance, and perhaps intimidate the Cubans a little.

The *Rio Escondido* had damaged her propellers when she ran into floating logs on her way from the US to Nicaragua and could make only five or six knots. In order that she arrive off Cuba at the same time as the other vessels, she left Puerto Cabezas on 12 April, three days before the first airstrike and a day before the main flotilla.

The landing craft *San Marco* which brought the Brigade tanks and artillery to the Bay of Pigs

USS *Essex*.

The rest of the fleet began weighing anchor at 5 p.m. on 13 April. The *Atlántico* went first, followed by the other ships. Legend has it that Luis Somoza, the Nicaraguan president, was standing on the quayside as they left, yelling at the men of Brigade 2506 to be sure to bring him back a bunch of hair from Castro's beard.

For the sake of safety and security the ships sailed independently, only coming together when they were twenty-five miles or so from the Bay of Pigs. This was no time or place for a convoy without escort. Much better and far less conspicuous to sail alone.

The men of Brigade 2506 hunkered down on the metal decks of the ships, only senior officers having been provided with cabins. The food was none too good, either, just cold rations from their packs. Some of the men were seasick and most were bored. They were all cold, shivering in discomfort and suppressed excitement as sea winds whipped in gusts across the decks, endlessly pulling the tops off the waves.

It was a relief for the men on the command ship *Blagar* when Pepe San Román tuned into Radio Swan. The Brigade soldiers gasped as they heard that Che

Guevara had been shot and killed during an argument in Fidel's office. There had been a coup and he had been removed from his post before the shooting, David Phillips reported. Phillips challenged Fidel to admit the fact. If it were not true he should present the famous guerrilla fighter in public.

There was an element of truth in the story – just an element. There had been no coup; Che was alive but he had been shot. At his military base on the western tip of the island he had dropped his revolver, the gun went off and the bullet grazed his face. He suffered a reaction to the anti-tetanus injection and during the three days of crisis was laid up in a medical centre. As a result he played no part in the Bay of Pigs affair.

The ships of the invasion fleet ploughed steadily onward, the men trying to keep up their spirits by cheering whenever a US destroyer was seen on the horizon. They played cards and listened to Radio Swan repeatedly broadcasting stories of battles between guerrillas and Castro's troops in the Escambray Mountains. Inevitably, with tension high, there were accidents.

On board the *Atlántico* an AA gunner accidently discharged his weapon. One man was killed and two wounded. When a US destroyer came alongside to take off the casualties the sense of depression that had hung over the men of Brigade 2506 since the accident was instantly distilled: the Americans were there for them and would always be there, whatever the problem.

Another shooting incident had occurred earlier when a soldier cleaning his rifle accidentally put a bullet into his own leg. Several Brigade members later suggested the man had done it on purpose and when he, like the victims of the AA accident, was also transferred onto a US ship for transportation to hospital others began to believe the rumours.

Along with grumbling about conditions, particularly the lack of hot food, the morale among the men of this 'liberation army' was not good. It seemed that the closer to action they came the more debilitating the tension.

As all members of the Brigade knew part of the invasion plan called for diversionary raids at various points along the Cuban coast. Their purpose was to distract the defenders and pull Castro's troops away from the real landing point. Two such raids were launched.

A few days before the main invasion, a force of nearly 170 men, led by Niño Diaz, was loaded onto the small transport *Santa Ana* and taken to the southeastern coast of Cuba. They were supposed to land twenty miles to the west of the US base at Guantanamo Bay and cause as much confusion as possible. Diaz, a veteran of Castro's 26th of July Movement, saw lights and troop movements along the coast and was immediately suspicious. A small reconnaissance team was landed to scout out the terrain and ascertain the strength of the Cuban defenders, as quoted by Rodriguez: 'Over and over again the scouts signalled that they could see many lights along the coast ... A little later the scouts came back and confirmed that military forces were there. The head of the battalion said that, in that case, the landing would have to be suspended.'

Diaz and his accompanying CIA case officer made a sensible decision. Each unit had been given a case officer, an advisor to represent the CIA position and give the American viewpoint in any debate. Now the two men decided to postpone the attack for twenty-four hours and the *Santa Ana* slipped out to sea where the watchers on the Cuban coast could not see or identify her.

On the second night, the *Santa Ana* returned to Cuban waters and the scouts were once more sent in. This time their speed boat managed to hit and lodge itself on a reef. Another launch was sent to tow the scouts back to the *Santa Ana*. During the rescue operation the sound of heavy vehicles along the coast confirmed that Cuban defenders were there in strength and Diaz refused to put his team ashore. If the Cuban defenders knew they were coming, he reasoned, a landing – one that was supposed to be a mere diversionary attack – would be nothing more than suicide. Instead he sailed westward and eventually arrived at the Bay of Pigs, too late to give any real assistance, before returning to Miami.

A second diversionary raid took place at Pinar del Rio at the western end of the island. This operation involved small boats fitted with loudspeakers and other equipment rather than large numbers of troops. The vessels cruised along the coast, transmitting what, to anyone listening on shore, were the sounds of a landing by heavily armed troops. Shots, shouted commands, motor engines being revved up, the cacophonic melodrama played out.

Both diversionary raids, the *Santa Ana* mission and the simulated attack at Pinar del Rio, were relatively successful. Large numbers of troops, militia and regular army were sent to the two areas where they saw no action and missed the real landings in the Bay of Pigs. They were soldiers that the Cuban army could have done with.

On the evening of 16 April, having rendezvoused with each other just twenty-seven miles from the Bay of Pigs, the invasion ships moved on to meet the *San Marco* off the Cuban coast. The *San Marco*, a relic of the Second World War, was a huge Landing Ship (Dock), carrying seven smaller landing craft inside its cavernous hull. These smaller vessels held the Brigade's tanks and trucks. The *San Marco* quickly flooded her afterdeck to launch the cargo and headed back to join the US Alpha Task Force some hundred miles off shore. Meanwhile the landing craft followed the invasion fleet into the Bay of Pigs.

That evening Pepe San Román and Manuel Artime held a short but moving ceremony on the deck of the *Blagar*. Artime spoke about Cuban history and the part that Brigade 2506 would play in it. The ceremony ended in a prayer. The grumbling and bitching stopped at that moment.

The fleet now split into two sections. The *Houston* and the *Barbara J*, carrying battalions 2nd and 5th, headed towards Red Beach, or Playa Larga, at the top of the bay while the other vessels made their way towards Blue Beach, or Playa Girón, the initial landing site for the 4th and 6th battalions.

Green Beach had never been intended to be more than a site for 3rd Battalion to protect the Brigade's right flank and for the moment it attracted little attention. In the event, on the advice of CIA case officer Grayston Lynch, the battalion

Playa Girón, scene of
the final battles.

eventually came ashore at Blue Beach. Pepe San Román was supposed to ferry them by lorry to Green Beach but it never happened and the battalion was subsumed into the Blue Beach force.

Grayston Lynch, like his counterpart Bill 'Rip' Robertson on Red Beach, was to organize setting the beach landing lights and to act as a trouble-shooter in case of serious problems. Those problems were just beginning.

Shortly after 1 a.m. on 17 April Pepe San Román led his soldiers down the ship's ladders on the side of the *Blagar* and into the landing boats. On the other freighters, now wallowing like humpbacked whales in the swells, the rest of the Brigade followed suit.

The night was pitch dark but ahead of them the men of Brigade 2506 could just pick out a single green light that had been set up by frogmen who had gone in an hour before to light the way.

The frogmen, a five-man underwater demolition team (UDT), had left the *Blagar* at midnight. At the last minute the UDT was joined by Grayston Lynch. A retired Special Forces operative, Lynch was deliberately ignoring the instruction that no US personnel were to take part in the landings. As he later stated, he felt that he needed to gain direct and first-hand knowledge of the situation on the beach before he could confidently order the landings to proceed. In reality as an ex-Special Forces man he could probably not resist the temptation for action once more.

Accompanied by a twenty-foot catamaran equipped with heavy machine guns, the UDT inched closer to the beach. Their boat was a navy inflatable powered by a silent motor and the men were armed with Browning Automatic rifles (BARs) and Thompson sub-machine guns. To the east the town of Playa Girón was ablaze with lights, Grayston Lynch later reported, but there was very little enemy activity. Problems came, however, when they ran onto a coral reef about fifty yards out from the shore. Thanks to aerial photography, dark shapes had been detected in the water some days before but US advisors insisted that these were nothing more than banks of seaweed. Now the frogmen cursed that if it was seaweed that they had hit then it was of a particularly solid type.

Stuck on the coral, the frogmen slid over the side of the inflatable and began to coax, pull and push their boat across the reef. Lynch remained in the inflatable, his BAR aimed menacingly at the beach.

Once over the obstacle the men crawled back into the boat and paddled to shore. There was a further problem when one of the red lights which were to be placed on the beach to indicate where Brigade 2506 should land, suddenly shorted and began to flicker.

'Sit on it,' Lynch ordered one of his men. 'Cover it up.' But at that moment the boat and the beach were bathed in blinding light. A jeep and two militiamen, part of the miniscule force defending Playa Girón, had arrived thinking that the frogmen were fishermen. They had come to offer their help but were quickly disabused of this idea when Lynch and his team opened fire. Over to the right the buildings of Playa Girón went dark as somebody threw the lights in the local power station.

The jeep lights also went out – shot out by the frogmen – and in very quick order the landing markers were set up on the beach. One of the militia soldiers was dead, the other running scared. When three trucks containing a squad of militiamen suddenly arrived a firefight erupted. The *Blagar* was now close inshore, preparing to unload her troops, and when her guns were added to the fire from Lynch and his frogmen, the militiamen melted away. They had not been eliminated, however, and these part-time soldiers were to offer more than just token resistance over the next few days.

By 4 a.m. men from the 4th and 6th battalions had begun to come ashore, many of them screaming out cries of success as soon as they hit the beach. It was, perhaps, a little premature as several of their landing craft promptly grounded themselves on the same coral reef that had caught Grayston Lynch and his frogmen.

The Landing Craft (Vehicle and Personnel) stuck fast and no amount of energy and effort could move them. The infantry had no option but to leave the vessels and wade ashore. They were soaked and, more importantly, so were their radios and ammunition.

With Pepe San Román taking control on the beach, Grayston Lynch now returned to the *Blagar*. He was met by heartbreaking news from CIA headquarters back in the US. Castro's air force, he was told, had not been eliminated and, inexplicably, there would be no further strikes against the airfields. The second part of the message was chilling: expect enemy air attacks at dawn.

It meant that all the invading infantry and their equipment would have to be ashore by first light or risk destruction from Castro's FAR. As Lynch knew only too well, ferrying troops ashore in the dark was an immensely difficult task. Cursing and fulminating at what he already realized was a bungled opportunity, the CIA man began doing what he could to hurry the landing.

The *Barbara J* and *Houston* arrived off Red Beach at Playa Larga soon after 1 a.m. Markers were placed by Rip Robertson and his frogmen but then they came under small-arms fire from militiamen hidden in the bushes that flanked the beach. When the demolition team returned fire the fusillade stopped. It was to start again as the troops began to disembark but by now the *Barbara J* was close enough to lend support.

Once Red Beach was secured the 2nd and 5th battalions moved on to clear the town of any remaining militiamen. The small militia unit fought desperately despite taking heavy casualties. At one point a bazooka shell from the Brigade smashed into a militia truck, killing twenty-one militiamen and a dozen civilians who had come to give the defenders what help they could.

The invading troops at Red Beach were under the command of Erneido Oliva Gonzalez, second in command to Pepe San Román, and to begin with at least seemed to be making reasonable progress. Unfortunately for them, however, the militia commander, before he and his troops were wiped out or captured, was able to pass on news of the landing to the command post at the nearby Central Australia Mill. A still-warm short-range radio – which, according to the CIA, the militia did not possess – had been used to pass on news of the landing. If President Kennedy and the Brigade commanders had hoped for a 'quiet' invasion the opportunity was lost.

It was during the initial action at Red Beach that the Brigade suffered its first D-Day casualty when one of the advance unit of frogmen was shot and killed. As at Blue Beach, underwater coral reefs posed something of a problem with the result that, as dawn began to break, considerable amounts of equipment and many of the 5th Battalion troops were still on board the *Houston*.

A Brigade landing boat with upbeat exile troops posing.

The CIA case officer for Red Beach, Bill 'Rip' Robertson, was a veteran of the Second World War and a man with a reputation for shooting first and asking questions later. Like Grayston Lynch, he was furious at the slow progress and knew that the margin between victory and defeat was tiny. Like Lynch he had gone with the advance force of frogmen to light the way to the beach but now he saw the chances of a successful landing slipping away.

Time was of the essence but nobody seemed too concerned. And then there were the technical issues that were more significant than anybody had expected. The so-called landing craft that were supposed to take the men of Brigade 2506 from the *Houston*, the *Rio Escondido* and the other ships into shore were soon found to be totally inadequate. In reality these vessels were no more than open-topped fibreglass boats powered by hopelessly inadequate outboard motors.

More importantly, the boats were too light to operate effectively in the swell and surf around the Cuban coast. Most of them immediately began to ship water and long before dawn only a handful remained in operation. At most they could take ten men; there were 400 to be disembarked on Red Beach alone.

Inevitably, there was the danger from the coral reefs that nobody seemed to have planned for. Even Erneido Oliva Gonzalez, ashore on the beach, began to fear the worst.

Meanwhile, thirty miles inland the paratroops of 1st Battalion began to drop from the C-46 transport planes. Commanded by Alejondro del Valle, these men had always regarded themselves as an elite part of the Brigade and now Operation Falcon, as the drops were known, would give them a chance to prove it. By 7.30 a.m. FAL aircraft had opened their doors and dropped 177 of them – with mixed success.

Thirty men came down south of the Central Australia Sugar Mill on the road to Playa Larga, some of them dropping directly into the Zapata Swamp. Even those who landed on dry ground saw their heavy weapons, ammunition and supplies disappear into the infamous swamplands. They attempted to retrieve them but most of the supplies were lost, with the result that, without ammunition or weapons, they failed to block the road to Playa Larga. It was a strategic disaster that meant government reinforcements could be sent in to attack the Brigade while it was still struggling to get off the beach, something that was to prove a decisive factor in the action to come.

Drops at San Blas, at Jocuma and at Horquitas went well, despite the paratroops landing amidst a large detachment of militia. Luckily the Brigade's airborne troops were more than able to hold their own. The roads across this part of the swamp were duly blocked and made unusable for Castro and his forces for two vital days.

Australia Sugar Mill complex, an essential mustering point for Castro's troops attacking down the road to Playa Larga.

Fidel Castro was informed that something big was happening at 3.30 a.m. He was spending the night in Havana with Celia Sanchez, one of his many lovers, and for perhaps the first time in several days he had managed to fall asleep. Dragged roughly back to consciousness, Fidel was told the news and immediately telephoned José Ramon Fernandez, commander of the military schools on the island. Fernandez was ordered to gather together 900 military cadets, the cream of the officer training programme, and proceed to the landing areas around the Bay of Pigs.

Castro's main concern, however, was not about the infantry battalions now coming ashore. He knew that without the support of rebels on the island their attack would soon flounder – and he had already locked up most of those who might be inclined to help. He had more than enough troops, regular army and militia, to deal with Brigade 2506. It was a fact that many in the US also knew and appreciated. In the words of US Secretary of State Dean Rusk: 'It was not necessary to call Price Waterhouse to discover that 1,500 Cubans weren't as good as 250,000 Cubans.'

For Castro the biggest threat came in the form of the ships that had brought the infantry battalions to his island. They could easily bring more men and equipment, they could also be used to evacuate them and therefore they had to be eliminated immediately. And for this, of course, he had his air force. He could hardly wait for morning to come.

Che and Fidel, a dynamic duo.

On the beaches around the Bay of Pigs the men of Brigade 2506 and their CIA organizers worked frantically. It was a herculean effort by all concerned.

By 7.30 a.m. all the Brigade's tanks were ashore as were many of the soldiers intended for Blue Beach, thanks partly to the efforts of Grayston Lynch who knew and understood only too well the importance of getting men ashore.

The alternative was to see those troops already on the beaches picked off and the ships, which were their only hope of salvation, destroyed by Castro's still-powerful air force. Unload and get away from the immediate beach area was how Grayston Lynch understood the situation.

For the men still coming ashore at Playa Larga, however, things did not look quite so rosy. The opposition was stronger and the road across the swamp to and from Central Australia Mill had not been blocked, meaning that there was always the threat of fresh defenders being shuttled in. For them it really was a battle against time.

And so they waited, the men of Brigade 2506, knowing that their future, and the future of the whole invasion, was in the balance. Then, finally, came the moment that they had all expected and each in their own way – Cuban exiles or Cuban defenders – dreaded or prayed for. First a gradual lightening and then, with all the glory of a firework display on 4 July, dawn burst suddenly in the skies over the eastern Caribbean.

7. THE PLAN UNRAVELS

'There seems to be something wrong with our bloody ships today.'
Admiral Beatty at the Battle of Jutland

The first aerial attack came at 6.30 a.m. Two Sea Furies and one B-26 of the FAR left San Antonio just before first light and arrived over Playa Larga twenty minutes later. There, in the brittle early morning sunshine, the jubilant crewmen were able to pick out the bulky shapes of the *Houston* and the *Barbara J* still unloading troops and supplies.

Piloted by Captain Carreras Rolas and Lieutenant Gustavo Bourzac, the Sea Furies immediately dived on the *Houston*. The first pass saw little more than huge columns of water climbing into the air as the bombs missed their target. Rolas was not the man to give up, however, and he attacked again, this time with rockets. One of them struck the supply ship on the stern and much to the pilot's delight, there was an immediate burst of flame. A third attack sprayed the ship with bullets before Rolas turned the nose of his Sea Fury and headed back to base at San Antonio to refuel and rearm. Lieutenant Bourzac took over the attack and his rockets also hammered into the now-disabled vessel.

Realizing that his ship was doomed, Captain Luis Morse knew that his only hope was to beach the *Houston* on the western side of the bay. He could not afford to let her sink as almost 180 members of the 5th Battalion and a large amount of supplies were still on board. Most of the Brigade's medical equipment was destroyed in the attacks, along with large numbers of weapons, but the task now was to get what was left ashore as quickly as possible.

Many of the soldiers, far too many of them without their weapons, went over the side and waded or swam to dry land. Some were taken to the beach using the *Houston*'s life rafts. Even so, it was late in the afternoon before everyone was on his native soil once more.

Unfortunately the survivors of the 5th Battalion had come ashore on the fringes of the Zapata swampland and according to their commander, Montero Duque, were not able to reach the fighting. Duque had already fatally delayed disembarking, declaring he was not prepared to send his men ashore until the landing area was secured and it was confirmed that Castro's troops did not have artillery. CIA case officer Rip Robertson, alternating between the beach and the deck of the shattered *Houston*, lost patience with him, convinced that the man had cold feet.

A captured Brigade tank. (Photo Alan Kotok)

Lynch recalled: 'Rip blew up. He told him, "Look, mister, it's your war and your country, not mine. If you're too scared to land and fight, then stay here and rot!"'

Shamed into landing, Duque made one half-hearted attempt to march toward Playa Larga. When his troops encountered half a dozen militia and some eager civilians they were halted in their tracks. On Duque's orders they turned back. Pepe San Román sent an urgent message commanding Gonzalez to relieve Duque of his post. When he was informed of this Duque's response was simply to turn off his radio. He did not inform his men of San Román's order but told them to dig protective trenches. They remained there until the rest of the Brigade surrendered two days later.

There was some initial success for the Brigade's air force on D-Day. Early that morning, as the landings were beginning, two FAL B-26 bombers caught the escort ship *El Baire* just off the Isle of Pines. It was thought she could be heading towards the Bay of Pigs to intercept the invasion fleet and so she was immediately attacked. Attempting to reach the safety of port the small vessel soon turned on her side and sank.

The FAL planes then swung round and headed for Playa Girón and the Zapata Swamp where they attempted to give support to the paratroopers on the far side of the morass. Ammunition and fuel low, they could manage only a few minutes over the beach and swamp before heading back to base.

The Escambray Mountains, traditional hideout for rebels. The Brigade was hoping to link up with anti-Castro rebels here. It never happened. (Photo Jane Gospel)

Throughout the day pairs of B-26 bombers were launched from Happy Valley on support missions but, in practice, this came down to aircraft appearing briefly over the beaches for little more than half an hour on each occasion. That left huge swathes of time with no air patrols to support the troops.

At 8.30 a.m., an FAR Sea Fury crashed into the waters of the bay. The Brigade, of course, claimed it was shot down by AA fire from one of the ships, the FAL stating it was due to air combat and the FAR believing that the pilot had simply stalled.

Such success was short-lived. At 9.30 a.m. three Sea Furies and a single T-33 were involved in a dogfight with FAL B-26s over Playa Girón. The aerial combat was largely inconclusive but then the FAR pilots spotted the *Rio Escondido* in the bay below. With the Brigade B-26s breaking off contact to head home to refuel and rearm, the FAR planes wheeled and dived at their new target.

Carrying drums of aviation fuel and ammunition on her deck, the ship was hit repeatedly by rockets and gunfire and was soon ablaze. The crew abandoned ship, some of them rescued by landing craft, the rest opting to swim for it. Within a few minutes the ship was rocked by three massive explosions and a mushroom-shaped fireball leapt into the air. The *Rio Escondido* sank like a stone and, for a brief moment, Rip Robertson over at Red Beach thought that Castro had detonated an atom bomb.

The ship went down with valuable food and medical supplies, as well as ammunition and fuel oil. Just as important, she took with her the radio caravan that gave the Brigade communications with the aircraft of the FAL and supporting fleet. Amazingly, there were no fatalities.

Throughout the operation, communication between Pepe San Román and Erneido Oliva Gonzalez was limited. Their short-range radios had been damaged by sea water and were working only sporadically. It meant that San Román could issue orders only to the troops on Blue Beach and, more importantly, he did not have any idea about what was happening to the men under Gonzalez command.

With the road from the Central Australia Sugar Mill still open, Erneido Oliva Gonzalez was already under huge pressure from the Cuban militia and military forces that were beginning to advance down the highway. Throughout the day reinforcements kept pouring in, marshalling at the sugar mill complex before heading for Playa Larga.

Gonzalez and his men fought a desperate battle but eventually they were forced to send a runner to the commander asking for infantry and tanks to help them plug the gap. Pepe San Román agreed and duly sent two M41 tanks, one recoilless gun and a number of infantry from the 4th and 6th battalions. They arrived at Red Beach in the early afternoon.

Cuban soldiers and militia.

In the skies above the landing beaches, the FAR aircraft were still causing havoc. At 11 a.m. an FAL B-26 was shot down by a Cuban T-33, the pilot surviving but the navigator being killed in the crash.

By the end of the day three more Brigade B-26s had been shot down, navigator Demetrio Perez being the only survivor from the three aircraft after he bailed out. He was picked up from the water by the US destroyer *Murray*.

Another B-26 suffered a different fate. It mysteriously disappeared after being damaged and diverted to Boca Chica. The remains of the plane and its crew were eventually found in the dense Nicaraguan jungle six months later.

It was the ships that were causing most concern. When CIA headquarters in Washington was informed by the men on the spot about the loss of two transport vessels there was a degree of panic. Lynch: 'an answer was received directing us to take all of the rest of the ships to sea and return and unload under the cover of darkness.'

It was a sensible decision as, during daylight hours, the freighters and large landing craft were just sitting ducks. After reassuring the men on the beaches that they were not being abandoned, the remnants of invasion fleet headed out to sea. Progress on their way out from the Cuban coast was tiresome and slow, the three surviving LCUs managing to make only six knots. And the FAR planes had not gone away.

Despite being in international waters the FAR pilots continued to harass the withdrawing enemy, pouring down rocket and machine-gun fire. Requests

Cuban forces attack near Playa Girón. (Photo Rumlin)

for air support from US forces were turned down. It was not all one-way traffic, however, and in one attack the *Blagar* gunners managed to bring down a Cuban B-26.

The plane hit the water just fifty yards from the ship and bounced forward, over the deck of the *Blagar*. The men on board were showered with wreckage but raced to the rail to watch the downed aircraft finally settle and sink some yards off the port quarter. FAR pilot Luis Silva Tablada, flying his second mission of the day, and his crew of three were all killed.

The captains and crew of the *Atlántico* and *Caribe* had been close to the beaches all day. These men were not professional soldiers schooled and trained in the ways of war: they were merchant seamen and the experience had been chilling. They had been bombed, seen the *Houston* and *Rio Escondido* destroyed and lived in imminent danger for hours on end. They had had enough.

When they finally managed to leave the Cuban coast behind them the two freighters simply kept on going. US destroyers, their crews knowing that both ships were carrying vital ammunition, managed to intercept the *Atlantico* a hundred miles out from Cuba. After some debate her captain was persuaded to swing around and return.

Playa Larga today. Little has changed. (Photo Susan Bollinger)

The *Caribe*, however, eluded the US Navy for over a day and was only caught when she was almost back at the mainland. There was no point turning her around – by then it was far too late.

Getting ammunition to the men on the beaches had now become vitally important. Airdrops from C-52 and C-46 aircraft met with limited success; dropping supplies onto tiny targets like Red and Blue beaches, bordered by the sea on one side and thick swamp on the other, was never going to be easy. Some supplies were retrieved but much was lost.

After midnight the *Blagar* and *Barbara J* managed to return and land some extra ammunition. It was something, at least, but everyone – on the ships and on the beaches – knew that it was never going to be enough.

The return of the *Blagar* was not without drama. The moment she began to turn back toward Cuba her engines stopped. In the engine room a group of survivors, picked up earlier from the *Rio Escondido*, had seized control. Lynch recalled: 'They announced that this was a mutiny. They indicated that they did not intend to take over the ship but were in control of the engine room and had no intentions of returning to Cochinos Bay to be sunk a second time.'

The mutiny was quickly crushed by Grayston Lynch's frogmen who stormed into the engine room and re-established control via the butt end of a few pistols.

Throughout the day hundreds of Cuban militia and regular army troops had been arriving, flocking to the Australia Sugar Mill, to Covadonga Mill and to Yaguaramas. Tanks, mostly Russian built T-34s that had served the Soviets so well in the winter campaigns of 1944, and heavy artillery were also transported to the combat zone.

The most tragic moment in the whole campaign came at midday. Hundreds of Cuban militia cadets, hastily assembled by José Ramon Fernandez as ordered by Castro, began to move down the road from the Central Australia Mill towards Playa Larga. Almost immediately the cadets, together with militia from the 339th Battalion, found themselves under heavy fire from Gonzalez's infantry and the supporting Brigade tanks. These were youngsters, some only sixteen or seven-

teen years old. They were brave, they were willing, and they were too young to die. They were annihilated. Those not killed fled into the undergrowth at the side of the road where they were able to find shelter of a sort. In Cuba the affair has always been called The Slaughter of the Lost Battalion.

Another assault along the road from the Central Australia Sugar Mill was launched by the militia just before 3 p.m. The militia were transported in open-topped trucks and trailers but by now San Román's reinforcements had reached Gonzalez and the men of Brigade 2506 were ready. Lynch again: 'The fire of the tanks and the recoilless guns, the 3.5s and the 12.7mm calibre machine guns of the landing force hit them before

Theatrical to a fault, particularly whenever there was a camera around, Fidel Castro leaps from one of his tanks.

they could get out of the trucks. This force was estimated at 1,500 and all the [Brigade 2506] survivors of this action [Bay of Pigs invasion] claimed they killed or wounded over half of them and destroyed most of the trucks.'

The Brigade may have overestimated its success but there is no doubt that the two actions on the afternoon of 17 April caused a considerable number of casualties among the Cuban militia. The Brigade also suffered a number of dead and wounded but, significantly, while the militia could afford to take casualties, Brigade 2506 could not.

Fidel Castro arrived at the Central Australia Sugar Mill at 4 p.m. He had spent the morning organizing troops and making a broadcast to the Cuban people, denouncing the invaders as mercenaries who had come to destroy the revolution and take away workers' right. At the Australia Mill Fidel met up with José Ramon Fernandez who had been battlefield commander for most of the day. Fidel brought with him the news that Osvaldo Ramirez, leader of rural resistance on the island, had been captured and immediately executed. It was immaculate timing, the news pleasing everyone. Castro then took over control of the defence. He was quick to issue orders and his enthusiasm affected others. Militia commander Rodriguez quotes: 'The people said "This won't last long, now that Fidel's come." Then he came here, to the sugar mill. While he was going around, he came up to me and I asked, "How are things going?" And he told me "Don't worry, pal; we'll finish them off in no time."'

Castro and his troops

By dusk Castro's forces were advancing from Cavadonga and Yaguaramas sugar mills. The Brigade troops at Red Beach found themselves under repeated attack – not from young boys any longer – and, inevitably, casualties mounted.

Ammunition began to run out and the Brigade slowly gave way. They had been fighting all day. They were tired and dispirited and they fell back. Eventually Gonzalez's troops found themselves where they had started the day, back on Red Beach.

Desperate to keep Castro's forces at bay, Pepe San Román decided to scrub the original idea of using tanks as infantry support. Instead, he ordered all the Brigade tanks and mortar squads to come together in defence of Red Beach.

At midnight the Cuban T-34s and the Brigade's M41s clashed. Castro's tanks had no option but to advance along the road in single file. They could not deploy across the swamp and the full weight of their armament could not be ranged against the enemy.

Newspapers all over the world trumpeted news of the invasion – this shows the front page of *Newsday*.

One of Castro's T-34 tanks, knocked out and in a ditch alongside the road.

The engagement was short and sharp. Commanded by Pepe San Román's brother Roberto, the Brigade tanks and the men of the Heavy Weapons Battalion gave a good account of themselves. Pepe later wrote that Roberto and his battalion caused more damage to Castro's forces than any other unit in Brigade 2506.

Six of Castro's T-34s were knocked out as, one by one, they came into range. Brigade tanks were also damaged but eventually the T-34s, fearing air attack, withdrew. It was estimated that the Cuban tanks and artillery had fired over 2,000 76.2mm and 122mm shells during the afternoon and evening and the invaders could only marvel at the amount of ordnance available to Castro's forces.

Despite what was soon being regarded as a Brigade victory the battle had also seen twenty exile soldiers killed and some sixty seriously wounded. It was the same with the armour. The Cuban tanks might have withdrawn but everyone knew they would be back, stronger and more numerous than ever. In contrast the Brigade's armoured units had no option but to stay and fight until they were either destroyed or ran out of fuel and ammunition.

In fact, the Cuban tank force was ready again at dawn on the second day, just a few hours after they withdrew. An extra ten T-34s and a number of IS-2M heavy tanks arrived from Central Australia Sugar Mill, a clear case of irresistible force suddenly meeting with an increasingly weakened enemy.

Shortly before 1 a.m. on 18 April, with the invasion now into its second day, Castro ordered another infantry attack. Both sides suffered heavy casualties but, eventually, shortage of ammunition forced Erneido Oliva Gonzalez to make a crucial, if unpalatable, decision. His troops would retreat to the beach and then move off along the coast road in order to link up with Pepe San Román at Playa Girón.

By now Castro had assembled a significant force to oppose the invaders. As well as 300 regular army soldiers there were 1,600 militia and 200 policemen – and that was after the losses of the previous day. There were also twenty T-34 and other tanks, as well as rocket launchers, artillery pieces and anti-personnel weapons.

With Erneido Oliva Gonzalez's men pulling out, the town of Playa Larga soon fell to Castro's infantry and there they paused. Meanwhile, Gonzalez prepared for the journey along the coast toward Playa Girón.

For Brigade 2506 D-Day had been long and the fighting tough, far tougher than anyone had ever expected. It was the determination of the Cuban defenders that surprised everyone. That, combined with a crucial lack of air cover, made a huge difference to the morale of the invaders, not just for the men on the ground but for the pilots as well. The decision not to proceed with air attacks on Castro's bases and planes had seriously demoralized everyone. Pepe San Román was later to comment: 'Our much needed and indispensable superiority in the air was converted into a suicide mission for Brigade pilots.'

With the failure to open up Girón airstrip there was little hope of effective air cover in the immediate future. When they had time to sit and consider the situation it seemed to the men of the Brigade that everything had been going wrong for them. The day had started well but it had quickly deteriorated. No matter how effectively or how long they fought, disaster always seemed to be hovering over the heads of the exhausted men. Two of the Brigade's supply ships had been sunk, a number of landing craft had been damaged or destroyed on the offshore reefs and ammunition levels – much of the reserve having gone down with the *Rio Escondido* – were dangerously low. There was to be little sleep for the men of Brigade 2506 that night.

8. AN ENDING

> 'Well, it seemed like a good idea at the time.'
>
> Steve McQueen, *The Magnificent Seven*

Daybreak on 18 April saw the invasion plan unravelling like threads on an old ripped jumper. Given the critical state of the Brigade's ammunition, the idea of a retreat toward the town of San Blas a few miles inland from Playa Girón was a sensible military decision. Psychologically, however, it was a disaster and the portent of utter failure descended like a shroud over Brigade 2506.

As soon as light returned to the Bay of Pigs, Erneido Oliva Gonzalez's men climbed wearily into their waiting trucks, taking most of their wounded with them but reluctantly releasing their prisoners. They all knew that it would not be long before these men would be back in action against them.

The Cuban militia, seeing the invaders pull out, immediately sent an ambulance to pick up the wounded – from both sides. Sadly, they also tried to sneak in two trucks full of militiamen in the wake of the ambulance. One of the Brigade's M41 tanks covering the withdrawal spotted them and quickly destroyed all three vehicles.

Cuban anti-aircraft gunners pose. In the days before Photoshop.

Playa Girón now began to assume a position of some significance. The road from the coastal village to Covadonga cut directly across the mud and wild grasses of the flanking marsh, one of the few routes across the otherwise impenetrable Zapata Swamp. Success or failure, victory or defeat for either side began to depend more and more on possession of the road.

When Erneido Oliva Gonzalez arrived at Playa Girón he found that San Román's forces, like his own, were desperately short of ammunition. He doubted they would have enough bullets and shells to withstand the next attack. Nevertheless, on San Román's orders, he took up position guarding the road from Playa Larga in order to prevent any attack from the rear. The main force under Pepe San Román was placed across and along the road outside San Blas. And there they waited.

In the early morning Fidel had been recalled to Havana when news came of another landing to the west of the city. Arriving in the capital he soon realized that this was nothing more than the second diversionary landing and so, without hesitation, he turned his jeep around and raced back to the Bay of Pigs. Once there he immediately took charge again.

Fidel was later scathing about the diversionary raids and the deception exercise involving Zuniga's B-26. Even Hollywood, he said, would not have tried to film such a feeble story. But the fact remains that he was pulled away from the action, albeit for a very short period of time, by one of these deceptions. As it happened there were no serious consequences but that was more by luck than judgement.

With their troops dispersed, San Román and Gonzalez discussed their options. It was clear that the invasion had failed and that no mass uprising would be taking place. Gonzalez suggested running for the Escambray Mountains and waging a guerrilla war. San Román was opposed to this idea and insisted that they should sit where they were and try to hold the beachhead as instructed. Pepe San Román, like so many other exiles, could not get it out of his head that the Americans would arrive soon. There was no way they would allow the Brigade to be wiped out. To San Román it was merely a matter of time before the US Marines would come pouring ashore.

When two US Navy Skyhawks suddenly swept across San Blas, the roar of their engines cracking the brittle stillness, it simply reinforced the notion that this was the start of American intervention. In fact the two planes, from the carrier *Essex*, were on a reconnaissance mission and had specific orders not to become involved in combat situations.

The previous day's landing at Playa Girón had been relatively unopposed, at least in comparison to the one at Playa Larga. But at 11 a.m. on 11 April, the

Cuban artillery towed into action by a bulldozer.

second day of the invasion, the expected confrontation began with a strong Cuban attempt to take San Blas. It was a crucial moment and Pepe San Román realized it.

He ordered the paratroops back from their forward position outside the town and these men, together with the soldiers from Playa Girón, managed to halt the offensive. Again, the cost in casualties and expenditure of ammunition was high. Realizing that his troops had failed to take the town Fidel ordered them to dig in and wait. In the meantime his artillery and aircraft would bombard the Brigade positions. All afternoon the shelling went on.

Meanwhile, back in Washington, President Kennedy was receiving news of the disasters with as good a grace as he could muster. Already there were stories, probably apocryphal, of the president crying in Jackie Kennedy's arms or pacing the floor of the Oval Office, bemoaning his bad luck and dreadful judgement. The one story that is probably true concerns old Joe Kennedy. Apparently JFK called his father for comfort and advice. Joe Kennedy responded in the only way he knew how: 'Oh Hell, if that's the way you feel give the job to Lyndon!'

At 2 p.m. on 18 April President Kennedy received a telegram from Premier Khrushchev of the Soviet Union. It was brief and to the point: the USSR would not permit US forces to land on Cuba. It was not stated but there was a clear implication that, if this happened, there would be a swift Soviet response with nuclear weapons.

With hindsight, given knowledge of the following year's events in Cuba, Khrushchev was undoubtedly bluffing, engaging in his familiar game of brinkmanship. But with disaster facing Brigade 2506 and with American involvement being made more obvious with every passing hour, it was the last thing Kennedy needed.

Khrushchev might have been playing games, Castro and José Ramon Fernandez were not. With the first assault on San Román's positions at San Blas having failed, they were desperate to finish off the invaders before nightfall. Fidel was angry that Gonzalez's forces had escaped from Playa Larga before he could attack them but they now seemed to be bottled up in the area around Playa Girón. It was too good a chance to miss.

In order to speed up the assault Fernandez ordered his men out of Playa Larga and onto the civilian buses that had brought them to the Bay of Pigs the previous day. Followed by trucks pulling artillery pieces and led by a column of tanks, the twelve Leyland single-deckers started out along the coastal road to Playa Girón.

At 5 p.m., as dusk was beginning to darken the Cuban countryside, they were caught at Punta Perdiz, midway between the two invasion beaches, by a flight of six FAL B-26 bombers.

With casualties and battle fatigue reducing the number of available Brigade pilots, Gar Thorsrud had given permission for two of the B-26s on this mission to be flown by Americans, something that pleased the Americans themselves and the exile flyers.

At first the militia cheered the B-26s, thinking that they were FAR planes – identification of FAL and FAR aircraft was a problem throughout the campaign – but then the aircraft opened fire. Machine-gun bullets, rockets and bombs rained down on the column. For the first time in the campaign napalm was used with the result that there were heavy Cuban casualties.

With orders to attack any troop concentrations on the road, FAR Sea Furies and T-33s which appeared over the road a few minutes after the FAL aircraft turned for home, also mistakenly fired on the column, succeeded in destroying one of their own trucks and killing many soldiers. It has never been clear how many Cuban troops died in the action but estimates vary between a hundred and a thousand.

Regardless of how many casualties they sustained, the Brigade air attack was serious enough for Castro to postpone his assault until the following morning. Shelling of the Brigade positions began again and continued all night, with Cuban 122mm guns pounding the battered exiles,

During the night of the 18th/19th two FAL C-46 planes finally managed to deliver arms and equipment to the combat-weary men of Brigade 2506, dropping supplies on the Girón airstrip and in the town itself. As ever, it was too little, too

Brigade troops in action

late. One B-26 did manage to land with some supplies early on the 19th, before it was really light, the first landing of the campaign at Girón airstrip. The plane could not afford the time to load badly wounded men who, it was decided, would be better left on the airfield.

However, the success of the airstrikes the previous evening led to a new FAL air operation being organized for 19 April. The exiles were demoralized and exhausted, a situation that led to US pilots being asked if they would be prepared to volunteer. In all, eleven American airmen put up their hands and volunteered for the mission.

These men were CIA contract pilots, mostly ex-military flyers who had been recruited by Major General Reid Doster of the Alabama Air National Guard. They had worked as trainers and delivery pilots for the Brigade; now they had the chance to do what they been trained for.

In what was later dubbed 'Mad Dog Flight', the last Brigade aerial mission of the invasion, two B-26s were shot down and four of the eleven American volunteers were killed. The unlucky men were Major Riley Shamburger, a former air force major, and his co-pilot Wade Gray. Like Shamburger, Wade Gray was a former air force man who had been working for the Alabama Air Guard. The other casualties were Thomas 'Pete' Ray, a pilot in the Air Guard and technical inspector for the Hayes Aircraft Corporation, and Leo Francis Baker, a former flight engineer at Hayes and who, when recruited, was managing a group of pizza parlours. Ray and Baker were shot down by a T-33 and crashed in a ball of flame on Girón beach. Amazingly, the two men survived the crash, only to be killed by the Cuban soldiers who, their blood lust up, were out to destroy anything that moved. Shamburger and Gray were hit as their plane approached Playa Girón. They were last seen, their aircraft at just under 100 feet, heading out to sea. They hit the water at 300mph.

There has been dispute over the deaths of Shamburger and Gray. Some reports say they were killed in the crash, others that they parachuted out of their burning plane only to be picked out of the water and immediately executed. A Cuban photograph – quickly withdrawn from circulation – showed both men lying dead on the beach with neat bullet holes in their foreheads. Regardless of how they died, four American flyers failed to make it back home.

All four men, technically civilians at the time of their death, were awarded the Distinguished Intelligence Cross, the highest honour bestowed by the CIA.

The end was now near for the men of Brigade 2506. A surprise, last-ditch attack on Castro's waiting troops by the Brigade's 3rd Battalion and by paratroopers was initially successful but it soon ran out of steam as the Cuban militia counterattacked.

The ensuing tank battle began at 10 a.m. and lasted until 2 p.m. The Brigade tanks managed to hold their own for a short while but then their ammunition began to run low and before long Castro's troops were finally able to occupy San Blas. Pepe San Román had no alternative but to order a retreat to the beach.

San Román and his men were now fighting with their feet in the water. The Cuban tanks were frighteningly close, even though several of them had been destroyed. When Brigade bazooka and mortar shells ran out, the Cuban tank commanders knew that they were untouchable. Police and militia

Riley Shamburger, one of the four US airmen killed on the final day of the invasion.

97

sheltered behind the tanks, emerging to engage in brief but effective firefights against an enemy that now had virtually nothing left to fight with.

Back in Washington President Kennedy was fighting a different type of battle. All evening on 18 April Admiral Arleigh Burke had been desperately trying to convince him to send in US planes to assist the Brigade. JFK was sticking to his plausible deniability theory and refused point blank. The president's biggest problem was that if he did send in troops they would have to win. There could be no possibility of the US losing and that would mean a significant intervention. And, of course, Khrushchev's recent telegram was a little too recent for comfort.

By nature a compassionate man, Kennedy was acutely conscious of the troops on the beaches. He also had the problem of the Cuban Revolutionary Council, the men who would soon, if everything went according to plan, become the rulers of the new Cuba. That eventuality was now virtually impossible but the Cuban Revolutionary Council remained.

The Council members were in a safe house at Opa-Locka outside Miami, guarded by US soldiers, waiting to be transported to Cuba. They had no idea what was happening on the island and to several of them the guards were there to keep them confined rather than protect them.

Arthur Schlesinger was sent to talk to them and explain the situation. Brought to the White House they were finally informed that the invasion was virtually over and that the emphasis now was to work out a rescue programme, as Schlesinger recounts: 'United States destroyers, with air cover and orders to fire if fired upon, were already searching the waters off the coast; Kennedy was prepared to run more risks to take the men off the beaches than to put them there.'

Cynically, rescuing men from the beaches and the water could be explained away as an act of humanity – unlike the cold-blooded hypocrisy that had put them there in the first place. But the council members were impressed by Kennedy's obvious sincerity, if not by the state of affairs on the beaches.

When they left the White House, the debates continued. In the early hours of 19 April, Kennedy finally gave in to Admiral Burke and agreed to provide US air cover of a sort. Six unmarked jets from the USS *Essex* would be permitted to fly over the beaches that morning in the hope that their presence would give the Brigade a degree of comfort and keep the FAR planes away. However, the jets would not be allowed to instigate aerial contests or attack targets on the ground unless they were, themselves, attacked. Timed to coincide with Mad Dog Flight, their role was to give moral support.

The men taking part in the Mad Dog Flight were overjoyed at what they saw as US intervention – at long last. In what was almost the final farcical moment in a tragic and ill-starred affair, the FAL planes took off too early and, as they swept over the *Essex* en route to Cuba, their crews saw the Navy Skyhawks lined up on the carrier's deck. The American pilots were sitting in their cockpits, waiting for orders to take off.

The Skyhawks were scrambled but by the time they were airborne the FAL planes had arrived over the beaches and were either in the process of being shot down or had completed their missions and were on their way home. The Skyhawks were too late to offer any assistance in the fighting.

The remnants of the Brigade had earlier been strafed by T-33s while a Sea Fury piloted by Enrique Carreras Rolas dropped bombs on Girón airstrip. They were the last missions flown by FAR pilots in the campaign as Castro ordered all air operations to halt that afternoon. The Brigade, he could see, was leaving the beach.

Launched too late and with instructions not to engage Castro's forces, the Skyhawks from the USS *Essex* played a negligible role in the invasion. (Photo Roger W)

At 3 p.m. Pepe San Román called his commanders together and ordered them to disengage from the enemy. They were to split into companies and move off into the swamp. There they would wait, in San Román's words, until 'Uncle Sam arrives'.

San Román was able to contact Grayston Lynch on the *Blagar*, asking once again for support. Lynch replied that there was none but that he could organize evacuation, using the landing craft. He urged San Román to accept the offer, to leave and fight another day. Pepe San Román was clear. He had come to free his country and had no intention of being lifted off the beach in ignominious defeat. A short while later his last message to Lynch was made: 'Am destroying all equipment and communications. I have nothing left to fight with. Am taking to the woods. Can't wait for you.'

The surviving Brigade members split into small parties, as ordered by San Román, and disappeared into the swamp and forests. Playa Girón was left

Brigade prisoners – the ultimate humiliation for men who had returned to free their country.

deserted but, littered with discarded equipment and uniforms, it had the sadness and the torment not of a battle lost or won but of one not really begun.

That afternoon two US destroyers appeared offshore. For the Cuban leaders it was a heart-stopping moment. They had fought and won: did the arrival of the American ships mean they had to start all over again?

In fact, the US vessels had come to rescue the Brigade. Several Brigade members were seen using small boats from the beach in an attempt to escape and with the destroyers lying just offshore it seemed an easy task to reach them.

José Ramon Fernandez ordered his artillery and tanks to fire at the boats but under no circumstances were they to attempt to engage the destroyers or do anything that would give the Americans an excuse to attack. The destroyer captains deliberated about firing back at Fernandez and his guns but in the end did nothing and soon withdrew from the bay.

Castro's troops entered Girón around 7 p.m., unopposed but wary of a trap. There was none: the Brigade had scattered, the invasion was over.

9. AFTERMATH

'Unarm Eros. The long day's task is done and we must rest.'

Shakespeare, *Antony and Cleopatra*

Defeat was a bitter pill for the men of Brigade 2506. They had returned to Cuba with belief in the righteousness of their cause. It now seemed as if the forces of darkness had prevailed.

During the night of 19/20 April another American destroyer, the USS *Conway*, arrived in the bay. Just under thirty Brigade members who had not left the area swam out to meet the destroyer's boats and were brought to safety' The 'night swimmers' were unusual. The vast majority of Brigade survivors took to the undergrowth and swamp, as Pepe San Román had ordered.

Castro was now desperate to catch these men. It became a political and military necessity to put them behind bars and he set up intensive search patrols, sweeping the area on foot and by helicopter.

The following day yet another destroyer, the *Eaton*, spent some time combing the shores of the bay for survivors, even pulling up alongside the remains of

The destroyer USS *Conway* returned to the Bay of Pigs looking for survivors. (Photo USN)

the half-submerged *Houston*. Joined by the USS *Murray*, the search went on for several days and in the end the destroyers managed to pick up twenty-six survivors. Search operations continued until 25 April and then the ships of Task Force Alpha retired to the Norfolk Navy Base in Virginia.

Over the next few weeks more and more members of Brigade 2506 were either captured or turned themselves in. The three leaders of the invasion – the two military leaders Pepe San Román and Erneido Oliva Gonzalez along with Dr Manuel Artime, the political head of the operation – managed to stay at large for a few weeks.

In the end lack of food and water – and a growing awareness of the hopelessness of their position – led to their inevitable capture. For the three men it was a bitter time. The Americans had not come to help and the feeling of betrayal was huge. At their resulting trial they were sentenced to thirty years in prison and ordered to pay compensation of $500,000 to the Cuban government.

The three were lucky. They could easily have been given the death sentence. A total of 1,224 members of Brigade 2506 were captured and incarcerated in Havana's Castillo del Principe to await trial. Nine of them died of asphyxiation while being transported to prison in the back of a closed army truck on a journey that should have taken two hours at the most but actually lasted nine.

Those men recognized as having served Batista – and there were more than a few in the Brigade – were immediately put on trial. Out of fourteen standing trial for crimes committed under the Batista regime, five were shot, the rest sentenced to thirty years in prison. These deaths were the tip of the iceberg. Castro's vengeance began almost as soon as the invasion attempt floundered.

More Brigade prisoners.

On 19 April seven Cubans and two CIA-hired American infiltrators, Angus McNair and Howard F. Anderson, were executed after a brief trial. Another infiltrator, Humberto San Marin, and five fellow guerrillas were executed on 20 April after being found with fourteen tons of explosives in their packs. Over the next twelve months there were hundreds of similar trials and executions that included the infiltration team leaders Antonio Diaz Pou and Raimondo Lopez and students like the underground leaders Virgilio Campaneria and Alberto Tapia Ruano.

Fidel was using the invasion to clean the stables. Anyone who might be likely to pose a threat to his regime was dealt with, the severity of the punishment varying with the likelihood of future disruption. Prison sentences were rarely less than thirty years and, of course, from the executioner's bullet there was no reprieve. Fines, like those levied against the leaders, were glibly given out although at that stage there seemed little likelihood of their ever being paid.

In total 114 members of Brigade 2506 died during and after the operation. That figure includes the nine men who died in the suffocating heat of a locked army truck. It also includes men who later died of their wounds and those Batista supporters who were summarily executed. It does not include any insurrectionists, infiltrators and guerrilla fighters captured and executed during and after the invasion.

The number and extent of Cuban army casualties remains unclear. With well over 100,000 army and militia troops involved in the fighting it was difficult to maintain exact figures, particularly regarding the militia. Large numbers of

JFK and Bobby Kennedy: their body language says it all.

civilians, many of whom had received basic militia training, rushed to join the defenders of their country and defeat the invaders. Many of them died in the process.

What is known is that 176 members of the Cuban army were killed, over 500 wounded. Figures for militia casualties vary but there could well have been over 2,000 killed. Other Cuban casualties – policemen, officer cadets and civilians – are estimated at between 500 and four thousand.

Four American pilots died in the invasion, six Cuban aircraft were shot down and six Cuban aircrew died. One Brigade paratrooper is known to have been killed and two of the CIA ships were sunk. One Cuban vessel was also sunk. Approximately 360 Brigade members were wounded, some seriously. Most of these wounded found themselves in captivity once the invasion failed.

Castro was aware of the value of the men he now held captive. In April 1962 he began negotiations for their release. In what was clearly a goodwill gesture, he sent sixty of the most seriously injured men back to the USA. Next he asked for 500 heavy-duty tractors, worth somewhere in the region of $28 million, in exchange for the men.

In December 1962 the lawyer James Donovan travelled to Havana to discuss the plight of the prisoners. They had been rotting in prison on places like the Isle of Pines for almost twelve months and it was high time something was done.

Lawyer James Donovan and Fidel Castro discuss the release of prisoners, December 1961. (courtesy Donovan family)

Donovan went to Cuba with the blessing of President Kennedy and on 21 December he and Fidel signed an agreement to release 1,113 Brigade members in exchange for $53 million. The 'ransom' was to be paid in medicine, agricultural equipment and food.

The first batch of prisoners was flown to Miami on 24 December; others made the journey by ship. Approximately 1,000 family members were also allowed to leave Cuba at the same time. The leaders like Pepe San Román were among the last to be released.

On 29 December JFK and his wife Jackie attended a large 'Welcome Back' ceremony at the Orange Bowl in Miami when Pepe San Román, Erneido Oliva Gonzalez and Manuel Artime presented the president with the Brigade flag. Kennedy promised that the flag would be returned when Cuba was free. Those Brigade members who remain alive are still waiting.

When the dust had settled it was clear that the Bay of Pigs disaster had caused the US government considerable embarrassment. The damage may not have been terminal – at least not for all of those involved – but it was enough to make the cynics smirk, the doubters shake their heads and even JFK's most fanatical supporters wonder what had gone wrong. The saving grace, however, was that there remained a surprising residue of goodwill toward the Kennedy administration.

Fidel Castro shows off the damage at Playa Girón to waiting cameramen.

Yes, there were demonstrations at college campuses across the US and a significant rally in Times Square on 21 April that drew a crowd of 3,000 protestors. Yes, there were pickets in front of the White House and yes, several writers and intellectuals condemned what they saw as a Kennedy-backed plot against a small nation. Mostly, however, the American people stood behind JFK, perhaps not agreeing with what had been done but prepared to give him a second chance.

Internationally, the criticism was considerably more virulent. Schlesinger: 'The New Frontier looked like a collection not only of imperialists but of ineffectual imperialists – and, what was worst of all, of stupid, ineffectual imperialists.'

Khrushchev and the Soviet Union, of course, adopted a gloating posture and even people like Konrad Adenauer of West Germany and Hugh Gaitskell of the British Labour Party – both of whom had welcomed the arrival of JFK after the torpor of the Eisenhower years – regretted the stupidity and the culpability of their American allies.

And yet, it was not all doom and gloom. In the strikingly apt words of British politician Dick Crossman: 'You really have got off very lightly ... If this had taken

Cuban AA gunners on post.

Victory assured, Fidel poses on a tank.

place under Eisenhower, there would have been mass meetings in Trafalgar Square, Dulles would have been burned in effigy, and the Labour Party would have damned you in the most unequivocal terms.'

Castro's popularity soared as might be expected in the wake of a humiliating defeat for the US. Everyone from the lowliest Cuban peasant farmer to the members of Fidel's government knew that the invasion was American-backed and for many Cubans it was as if they had defeated the US Marines, Army and Navy, all at the same time. Dalleck noted: 'Under Secretary of State Chester Bowles commented that a failure "would greatly enhance Castro's prestige and strength." And Bowles saw the odds of a failure as two to one.'

Fidel Castro might have been revelling in his increased popularity but he was aware that the danger had not passed. In the wake of their humiliating defeat he confidently expected a further American attack. To counter that he needed allies and the most likely and effective ally he could find was the Soviet Union.

To misquote Charles Dickens's Mr Barkis, Khrushchev was willing, Castro was willing and so it was inevitable that with the failure of the Bay of Pigs invasion the two left-leaning powers were pushed naturally together.

Weapons were soon flooding into Cuba and by the summer of 1962 it was not just conventional guns, aircraft and rockets but nuclear missiles and warheads that were making their way from the Black Sea ports to the Caribbean island.

Perhaps inevitably, given the animosity between the CIA agents and the men of the Brigade, there were grumblings and accusations of cowardice thrown at the Cuban exiles. The fact that almost 1,200 of them had been taken prisoner rather than suffer a glorious death on the battlefield, many CIA men thought, was proof positive that the Brigade lacked guts and determination.

The 'welcome back' rally in Miami. Artime takes the salute.

It was a facile attitude, patently untrue except in a few cases – something that inevitably surfaces in all military campaigns – and one that even Fidel Castro was at pains to discredit: 'The invading forces fought very well as long as they thought they had air cover. After it failed, it was an easy matter to get them to surrender.'

During his captivity Pepe San Román met Castro several times. In his book *Rebuttal* – written in response to a critical article in the *Miami Herald* – he recorded that Fidel had told him he originally thought that he was facing a skilful, well-prepared force of over 10,000 men. It may have been Castro seeking to console a defeated opponent but, in the prison cell, the Cuban leader was adamant that 'he could not deny the admiration that he felt for the men under my command'.

The Bay of Pigs invasion, its build-up and its aftermath, was perhaps the moment when Fidel and Che Guevara, bosom buddies from their days as guerrilla fighters in the hills, stood closest together. For years the Cuban people and the world had viewed them as one entity, two men who fought, lived and defied death together. Of course that was an image, one that was carefully designed and maintained by Che and Fidel, but that was how they had always been seen.

Even though Che had played no real part in defeating the invaders, Fidel certainly had. He had led from the front, often sitting in a tank directing its course – while writing out his next government edict. He had been in his element. It was not as if he suddenly discovered he could do without the flamboyant Che, the change if anything came from Guevara.

He and Fidel had stood side by side for years but this crushing of capitalist forces now made Che feel that this was the end of an era. The revolution had been consolidated and its success assured. There were other countries that needed attention and within a few years he had moved on to Bolivia in order to foment more revolution. It was a task or a calling to which he was drawn and it led, eventually, to his death.

There were few crumbs of comfort for the Kennedy administration. As the dust settled on the Bay of Pigs, the problem of civil rights and the Freedom Riders in the Deep South reared its head. Both JFK and Bobby became immersed in that issue until the Missile Crisis of 1962 brought them sharply back to the problem of Fidel Castro.

If there was one good result from the Bay of Pigs invasion, however, the disaster finished Kennedy's love affair with the espionage world. As an avid reader of Ian Fleming's James Bond novels – along with Jackie, brother Bobby and, seemingly, the entire staff of the White House – he had invested the spy world with an aura of glamour that was patently untrue. He had even met the sophisticated

English writer and asked his advice about dealing with Cuba. Quite what Fleming thought about this remains unclear.

After the Bay of Pigs débâcle, things changed dramatically. The CIA in particular was now viewed with open suspicion and dislike. David Talbot expanded: 'It [the Bay of Pigs affair] would abruptly terminate JFK's romance with the spy agency, turning the Kennedy brothers and their national security apparatus explosively against one another.'

Put simplistically, JFK turned from the cigars and martinis, the whole gadget-laden world of Fleming, to the bitter reality of John Le Carré – the analogy is out of time chronologically but is an apt way of describing the change. In the future JFK would rely on his own judgement, taking advice from an experienced and able group of individuals like his brother Bobby, Ted Sorensen and Robert McNamara.

In the meantime there was the damage to America's prestige to deal with. Raúl Castro, like his brother Fidel and Nikita Khrushchev, looked at the events and decided that Kennedy was weak – 'flaky' as a future US president would have put it. In a 1975 interview for a Mexican magazine, Raúl commented that 'Kennedy vacillated. If at that moment he had decided to invade us, he could have suffocated the island in a sea of blood, but he would have destroyed the revolution. Luckily for us he vacillated. If, instead of Kennedy, we had had any of the later presidents they would have intervened and destroyed the revolution.'

Not anymore. From now on Kennedy would ply a different course. Failure at the Bay of Pigs was the forerunner – maybe even the cause – of the Cuban Missile Crisis of 1962. And as that crisis loomed the universal hope of all national leaders was that JFK had learned from his mistakes – that is, all national leaders apart from Castro and Khrushchev.

Disabled Bay of Pigs veterans listen to an address by JFK. One wonders how sceptically.

Ted Sorensen, JFK's advisor and speechwriter, who would go on to play a significant role in the Cuban Missile Crisis.

There was always something of the clown or the buffoon about Castro – perhaps that was why he and Nikita Khrushchev got along so famously. But like Stalin before him, Fidel underestimated the decency and the humanity in the soul of the Soviet leader so that, a year after the Bay of Pigs, when the ultimate crisis arose it was Khrushchev who stepped back from the brink. Castro wouldn't have done it nor JFK if it had come to the push.

They had learned that inflexibility from the Bay of Pigs disaster. Khrushchev was willing to look weak and slightly silly if it preserved humanity. Dictators like Castro and Stalin, it seems, invariably underestimate the opponent who is willing to look foolish. Not to mention decent democratic leaders like John F. Kennedy.

10. FINDING THE CAUSES, ALLOCATING BLAME

'A Dothraki wedding without at least three deaths is considered a dull affair.'
George Martin, *A Game of Thrones*

The Bay of Pigs invasion was probably the most ill-conceived, badly planned and poorly organized military operation of the twentieth century. And when it was over reasons for the disaster had to be found. So, too, were scapegoats.

Within two days of the Brigade surrendering Kennedy ordered an inquiry. As president he knew he had no alternative but to accept the responsibility for the failure, echoing Harry Truman's message that 'the buck stops here'. But there had been others more directly involved than him in what had become a long and costly failure.

Chaired by General Maxwell Taylor, former Army Chief of Staff, the Cuba Study Group (or the Taylor Committee as it became known) was made up of Taylor and three others: Admiral Arleigh Burke from the Joint Chiefs of Staff, Allen Dulles from the CIA and the president's brother, Bobby Kennedy. It was an interesting if not exactly impartial group. All of them apart from Taylor had been involved in the affair almost from the beginning.

On Saturday 22 April, less than a week after the first members of Brigade 2506 had landed at the Bay of Pigs, the Taylor Committee met for the first time. The meeting lasted for just four hours and, as might be expected, there was a heavy CIA presence. Over the next

General Maxwell Taylor who led the first investigation into the disaster.

three weeks the committee came together on twenty-one occasions and collected an enormous volume of material, presenting its preliminary report to JFK on 16 May.

Evidence was taken from the Joint Chiefs of Staff, from Cuban exiles and from CIA officers of various rank and standing. If it was not exactly a 'snow job' there was a tacit understanding that certain individuals had to be protected.

Taylor himself commented that Bobby Kennedy, the Attorney General, could be counted on to look after the interests of the president while Dulles and Burke would make sure that no damage would be incurred by the CIA and the Chiefs of Staff. And so it proved, Jack Pfeiffer writing that 'After his "mea Culpa" and acceptance of responsibility for the operations, the President and his less than squeaky clean coterie escaped all blame for the invasion's failures; but the CIA has continued to bear the full brunt of responsibility for the "fiasco" at the Bay of Pigs.'

President Kennedy's responsibilities for the disaster lay in two areas. The most significant was the cancelling of airstrikes against the still-active Sea Furies and T-33 fighters on D-2, D-1 and in particular on D-Day itself. Rather than wiping out the FAR before it could get into the air, the FAL aircraft were reduced to a support role for the infantrymen now coming ashore – for which they were clearly unsuited. The president was aided in making this poor decision by Charles Cabell, Deputy Director of the CIA. In the absence of Allan Dulles, who was away in Puerto Rico, the ultimate decision-making for the agency lay in his hands. Cabell was dramatically and criminally unclear how many strikes had been planned and authorized. He had an idea that it was just one, something which Kennedy soon confirmed. It was poor communication and dreadful decision-making.

Changing the invasion beaches from Trinidad to the Bay of Pigs was another Kennedy blunder. The Zapata Swamp was isolated, leading Bissell to the belief that thanks to its poor communications with Havana, the men of Brigade 2506 could be ashore, the Girón airstrip captured and the new Cuban government flown in before Castro knew what was happening. He was wrong, as the militia attacks and defence of Playa Larga and Playa Girón showed.

More importantly, the Zapata Swamp and the landing beaches were too far away from the Escambray Mountains, thereby excluding any possibility of a guerrilla campaign or the linking up with insurgents on which the whole operation depended. Equally as significant, there was no possibility of survivors taking to the hills if anything went wrong.

None of this was possible once the landing site was changed from Trinidad to the Bay of Pigs. Kennedy and his advisors were unclear, even confused, about the option of guerrilla operations if the situation at the beachhead became untenable.

Charles Cabell, Deputy
Director of the CIA under
Allen Dulles.

It was an assumption, just like the belief that the Americans would step in to help out was an assumption.

General Lemnitzer, Chair of the Joint Chiefs of Staff, in his evidence to the Taylor Committee stated that the only plan for withdrawal was by sea. There was no possibility and never any intention of Brigade members escaping to the hills to hide or fight as guerrillas.

Inevitably, the shadow of plausible deniability hung over almost every decision the president made during those few short days. He had clearly not promised US aid on the beaches or in the air but the men of Brigade 2506 thought that he had. Like Dwight Eisenhower before him, Kennedy would do nothing to show the American hand. The men of Brigade 2506 could be forgiven for thinking that they had been abandoned and betrayed.

The most significant of all these blunders, of course, was the cancelling of airstrikes against the FAR, particularly when it became known that very few of Castro's T-33s and Sea Furies had been destroyed in the one raid that the FAL had been allowed. As the CIA conceded, cancelling the D-Day strike

General Lyman Lemnitzer of the Joint Chiefs of Staff.

in particular was significant 'as it eliminated the last favourable opportunity to destroy Castro's air force on the ground'.

One of the criticisms levelled by the Brigade participants was that the US controlled everything but when the chips were down they did nothing to help. If the invasion had been Cuban-planned and Cuban-run they felt it would have been a lot more successful. Being controlled by Washington did not sit easily with these exiles.

At the end of the discussions and after interviewing sixty witnesses – strangely, though, not including people like Howard Hunt, Tracy Barnes and Gerry Droller – the Committee came down to four reasons for the failure:

1. A lack of early realization that success was impossible.
2. Inadequate air cover before and during the invasion.
3. Limited armaments for the men on the beach.
4. Plausible deniability.

Several of these charges – particularly the old chestnut of plausible deniability – could be laid at the door of JFK. But they weren't. That would have been too painful for everyone concerned and the implicit message was that it was the CIA that would shoulder the blame.

Allan Dulles had given evidence on the last day of the investigation. He was a poor witness, stating that he was taken by surprise by the effectiveness of Castro's air force, in particular the T-33s which he understood to be nothing more than unarmed training aircraft. This was untrue. The fact that each of the T-33s was armed with two .50-calibre machine guns was well known in CIA headquarters.

Like the president, Dulles had the good grace to admit at least some of his faults. As far as he was concerned his major error was not being accessible when the invasion took place. He was away from Washington giving a speech to a Young Executives group in Puerto Rico and to cancel something that had been in his diary for over a year, he declared, would simply draw attention to American involvement.

He had a list of excuses for his other failings. One he could not deny or skirt around was his failure to tell JFK and Eisenhower that the change from guerrilla tactics to a standard beach landing had, in a moment, destroyed the concept of plausible deniability. Armed with this knowledge Kennedy could have made a decision – drop the whole idea or go in with a full US-led invasion, something the Chiefs of Staff and others had been urging for months.

At the end of 1961, Lyman Kirkpatrick, Inspector General of the CIA, also carried out an investigation into the disaster. If Taylor had been concerned with protecting Kennedy, then the CIA's own internal investigation was intent on denigrating Richard Bissell. It was time to hang out the Deputy Director for Plans and leave him there to dry. If Allan Dulles was go to the wall in the same bloodbath that was fine and dandy, too.

Kirkpatrick came up with nine reasons for the failure, some of them covering the same ground as the Taylor Inquiry but all highly critical of the CIA:

1. The CIA exceeded its capabilities in changing the attack from guerrilla operations to a full scale assault, thereby destroying the concept of plausible deniability.
2. A failure to assess risks and communicate information.
3. Insufficient involvement of Cuban exile leaders.
4. Failure to organize effective resistance within Cuba.
5. Failure to collect and analyze information about the Cuban forces.
6. Poor internal management.
7. Insufficient Spanish speakers during training.
8. Not enough high-quality staff involved.
9. Lack of contingency plans.

As an analysis of the invasion and the reasons for its failure Kirkpatrick's report was condemnatory. Above all, he believed: 'The failure was due to the breakdown of communications between the CIA and the DOP [Director of Plans] on the one side and the White House, the President and his cohorts on the other.'

Allan Dulles and Richard Bissell dutifully tendered their resignations. Dulles was at the end of his career anyway but it was a sad and ungenerous way to leave a post he had held for years. For Richard Bissell, an ambitious man who had harboured hopes of eventually leading the CIA, it spelled the end of what he always described as the best years of his life.

Dulles and Bissell were not the only ones to fall on their swords. Charles Cabell, Dulles's deputy in the CIA, was also gone by January 1962. Cabell had been deputy at the CIA since 1953 but his lack of judgement regarding the offensive airstrikes

CHART OF COMMAND ORGANIZATION FOR OPERATIONS

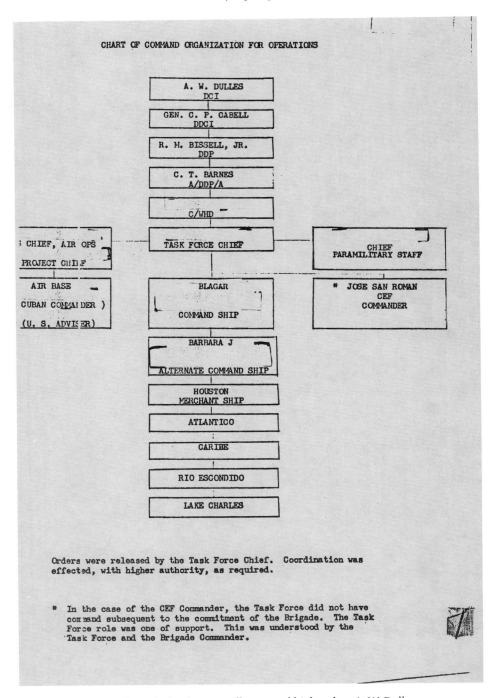

A. W. DULLES
DCI

GEN. C. P. CABELL
DDCI

R. M. BISSELL, JR.
DDP

C. T. BARNES
A/DDP/A

C/WHD

CHIEF, AIR OPS
PROJECT CHIEF

TASK FORCE CHIEF

CHIEF
PARAMILITARY STAFF

AIR BASE
CUBAN COMMANDER)
(U. S. ADVISER)

BLAGAR
COMMAND SHIP

* JOSE SAN ROMAN
CEF
COMMANDER

BARBARA J
ALTERNATE COMMAND SHIP

HOUSTON
MERCHANT SHIP

ATLANTICO

CARIBE

RIO ESCONDIDO

LAKE CHARLES

Orders were released by the Task Force Chief. Coordination was effected, with higher authority, as required.

* In the case of the CEF Commander, the Task Force did not have command subsequent to the commitment of the Brigade. The Task Force role was one of support. This was understood by the Task Force and the Brigade Commander.

In this organization chart, the buck eventually stopped higher than A. W. Dulles.

Department of Justice

OFFICE OF THE
RECEIVED
APR 24 1961
ATTORNEY GENERAL

April 20, 1961

Statement by Attorney General Robert F. Kennedy

There have been a number of inquiries from the press about our present neutrality laws and the possibility of their application in connection with the struggle for freedom in Cuba.

First, may I say that the neutrality laws are among the oldest laws in our statute books. Most of the provisions date from the first years of our independence and, with only minor revisions, have continued in force since the 18th Century. Clearly they were not designed for the kind of situation which exists in the world today.

Second, the neutrality laws were never designed to prevent individuals from leaving the United States to fight for a cause in which they believed. There is nothing in the neutrality laws which prevents refugees from Cuba from returning to that country to engage in the fight for freedom. Nor is an individual prohibited from departing from the United States, with others of like belief, to join still others in a second country for an expedition against a third country.

There is nothing criminal in an individual leaving the United States with the intent of joining an insurgent group. There is nothing criminal in his urging others to do so. There is nothing criminal in several persons departing at the same time.

What the law does prohibit is a group organized as a military expedition from departing from the United States to take action as a military force against a nation with whom the United States is at peace.

There are also provisions of early origin forbidding foreign states to recruit mercenaries in this country. No activities engaged in by Cuban patriots which have been brought to our attention appear to be violations of our neutrality laws.

Bobby Kennedy discusses neutrality after the fact

against Castro's FAR – even though limiting these was a plan conceived by JFK – led to the president forcing him to resign. Long-term memory was not one of the strengths of White House politicians.

Interestingly, Cabell's brother Earle was mayor of Dallas when Kennedy arrived in Texas on his fatal trip in 1963. For a brief period there was a theory that Charles and Earle Cabell had conspired to assassinate the president to get their own back. It was a knee-jerk notion, an idea that went nowhere and was soon dropped.

Admiral Arleigh Burke, Chief of Naval Operations, the man who had tried so vociferously to get Kennedy to send in navy aircraft in the final stages of the operation, was also out of government service by the end of the year. His demise might have had something to do with a ridiculous comment he made: 'The D-2 strikes were not designed to knock out any great amount of the Cuban air force. This was to be done by the D-Day strikes.' Burke was either being 'arch' or particularly naïve. Either way it was an abysmally ignorant statement to make, particularly after the D-Day strikes were cancelled.

Other advisors or serving officers luckily remained in post. Men like Ted Sorensen, Kennedy's scriptwriter, and National Security Advisor McGeorge Bundy kept their jobs. Bobby Kennedy, of course, was never in any danger.

Hard-talking General Curtis LeMay was actually promoted, soon succeeding General White as Air Force Chief of Staff. He remained in post to become a major thorn in Kennedy's side during the Cuban Missile Crisis the following year.

Whatever else he was, LeMay was a shrewd operator and saw immediately that the invasion force would need air cover. He was also hard-headed enough to speak out about his concerns.

The one person who was, perhaps, lucky to keep his job was Secretary of Defense Robert McNamara. At some stage during the crisis he managed to 'lose' two important papers from the Chiefs of Staff. They were reports that represented the thinking of the chiefs at that time.

One suggested that an inter-departmental group should be formed with the aim of ousting Castro. The US military would, naturally, play the most significant role. The second paper stated that the original plan of the CIA was markedly better than the alternative move to the Bay of Pigs. Neither of the reports contained facts that Kennedy wanted bandied around at that time so perhaps he and McNamara were engaged in a cunning, long-play game. It makes interesting speculation.

Either way, those who stayed were vital in the months and years ahead. All of them played significant roles in the Missile Crisis of 1962. The Bay of Pigs affair battle-hardened them, ready for what was to come.

CONCLUSION

'When the legend gets bigger than the truth, print the legend.'
Newspaper editor in *The Man Who Shot Liberty Valance*

With emotions remaining high, rumour, legend and truth inevitably became mixed in the years after the failure of the invasion. In December 1962 Pepe San Román, perhaps looking for excuses, perhaps taken in by political duplicity, was convinced of higher influences at work: 'The President explained that after the first airstrike on April 25th [D-2] the Russian government threatened an attack on West Berlin if the United States continued to assist the invading forces commanded by me.'

A Soviet assault on Berlin was JFK's great fear, both in 1961 and during the Cuban Missile Crisis of the following year, but such a move was never explicitly stated. Hinted at, yes, but the threat was always implicit rather than hard reality. Nevertheless, it suited Pepe and Kennedy, both coming from different positions, to believe that it had.

As originally devised the invasion of Cuba might have had a chance of success. Once arrangements were changed it should have been immediately obvious to everyone that the men of Brigade 2506 were facing disaster.

The inability of the organizers to provoke a rising on the island, the inaccessibility of the Bay of Pigs and, above all, the lack of adequate air cover combined with an effective Castro-run air force closed the door on whatever chances the exiles might have had. Those are incontrovertible facts.

In Cuba, however, the bravery of the men who defeated American plans has always been more significant than American mistakes. They deserve their moment of glory, those militiamen. It was an achievement of some style. But then, so too do the soldiers of Brigade 2506. They fought overwhelming odds with little support and they, like the Cuban militia, are deserving of their fame. They carry with them the tragedy of glorious failure – and that has always had a certain appeal.

So many of the principal players have now left the stage for good. Both Kennedy brothers, Fidel, Che, even Pepe San Román who committed suicide in 1989, they have all died, some violently, some peacefully in their beds. It hardly matters – the point is that so many of the men involved in the Bay of Pigs disaster are no longer around to tell their tales.

That is one reason why the story needs to be told, in full, not as a mere mention or a footnote in books that have a broader sweep.

Members of the Brigade resumed their normal lives once released from prison. But they never forgot their fallen comrades or their desire to see Cuba free once again.

The Bay of Pigs disaster was a precursor, almost a warm-up act, for the greater dangers that were to come in the year ahead. That should not detract from the courage and the skill, even the foolishness and stupidity of the men involved. They took part in a moment of history and they did it with pride and appreciation. That should never be forgotten.

The cancellation of airstrikes on D-1 and D-Day effectively condemned the Bay of Pigs invasion to disaster. And yet the members of the Brigade went ahead with the assault, many of them knowing, before they even went ashore, that only death and failure were waiting for them on the beaches of Playa Larga and Playa Girón.

The final words belong to the Cuban exiles. In his foreword to Pepe San Román's *Rebuttal* Alberto Martinez Echenique succinctly summed up the beliefs and attitudes of many members of Brigade 2506: 'After promoting, funding, organizing, assisting and escorting it [the Brigade] in its efforts to invade, the Government of the United States of America, due to political reasons of state, actually abandoned the project before 17 April 1961.'

SOURCES

Books

Anon, *The Bay of Pigs Invasion*, Charles River Editors, London, undated

Carey, John, *The Faber Book of Reportage*, Faber, London, 1987

Carradice, Phil, *The Call Up*, Fonthill, Stroud, 2016

Dalleck, Robert, *John F. Kennedy: An Unfinished Life*, Allen Lane, London, 2003

Dobbs, Michael, *One Minute to Midnight*, Arrow, London, 2008

Hanhimaki, Jussi & Westad, Odd Arne, *The Cold War*, Oxford University Press, Oxford, 2003

Lynch, Grayston, *Decision for Disaster*, Potomac Books, Washington, 2009

Rasenberger, Jim, *The Brilliant Disaster*, Scribner, New York, 2011

Reid-Henry, Simon, *Fidel and Che*, Hodder, London, 2008

Rivas, Santiago, *Playa Girón*, Helion & Co., Solihull. 2016

Rodriguez, Juan Carlos, *The Bay of Pigs and the CIA*, Ocean Press, New York, 1989

San Román, José 'Pepe; Perez, *Rebuttal: The Truth about Girón*, Bay of Pigs Museum, 2014

Schlesinger, Arthur M., *A Thousand Days*, Fawcett Crest, New York, 1967

Selsden, Esther *Castro*, Parragon Press, London, 1994

Talbot, David, *Brothers*, Simon & Schuster, London, 2007

Reports

Internal Investigation of the Bay of Pigs, Doc No 0001254908, originally entitled 'An Analysis of the Cuban Operation' by the Deputy Director (Plans), Central Intelligence Agency

Official History of the Bay of Pigs Operation, Vols I to V, Central Intelligence Agency

Pfeiffer, Jack, 'The Taylor Committee of Investigation of the Bay of Pigs', 9 October 1984

Internet

https:en.wikipedia.org/wiki/1954-Guatemalen-coup

https:en.wikipedia.org/wiki/Bay-of- Pigs-Invasion

www.aewsomestories.com

www.bbc.co.uk/news/world-latin-america-13066561

www.cia.gov/news-information/featured-story-archive/2006
www.encyclopedia.com/latin-america-and-caribbean/Cuban-history/bay-of-pigs
www.history.com/topics/cold-war/bay-of-pigs-invasion
www.historyextra.com/article/bbc-history-magazine/bay-pigs-invasion-why-fail-kennedy-cuban-catastrophe
www.historyonthenet.com/the-bay-of-pigs-invasion
www.jfklibrary.org/JFK-in-history/the -Bay-of-Pigs.aspx

Periodicals

BBC World Histories article 'Did the Cold War Ever Really End?'
Miami Herald
The New York Times
The Guardian, 23 December 2014
The Spectator, Charlotte Hobson article, 10 June 2017

Playa Girón. (Photo Gorupdebesanez).

ACKNOWLEDGEMENTS

Many people helped in the writing of this book: My old friend Roger MacCallum who, with his command of technology, was always willing to help a confirmed Luddite out of his self-dug pit. My youngest son Douglas for some intriguing additions to the chapter sub-titles. Andrew, Helen, Anne, Lewis, Judith and Lennie for your continued support and encouragement. Jack, my grandson, whose regular orders to 'Come and play' stopped the writing becoming a chore and enabled me to return to the MS – usually after a takeaway – with a fresh eye every time. Trudy, always in my head and at my shoulder, even though you have been gone for nearly two years now. Inspiration never dies, sweetheart.

The Bay of Pigs
memorial in Miami.
(Photo Infrogmation)

INDEX

Index

ABOUT THE AUTHOR

Phil Carradice is a poet, novelist and historian. He has written over fifty books, the most recent being *The Call-up: A Study of Peacetime Conscription in Britain and Napoleon in Defeat and Captivity*. He presents the BBC Wales history programme *The Past Master* and is a regular broadcaster on both TV and radio. A native of Pembroke Dock, he now lives in the Vale of Glamorgan but travels extensively in the course of his work. Educated at Cardiff University and at Cardiff College of Education, Phil is a former head teacher but now lives as a full-time writer and is regarded as one of Wales's best creative writing tutors. He writes extensively for several Pen & Sword military history series including 'Cold War 1945–1991' and 'A History of Terror'.